SURPRISING MIND BLOWING
FACTS AND FIGURES OF BIG DATA

Ajit Kumar Roy

Copyright Page

DEDICATION

The book is dedicated to
my granddaughter
'ANGANA'

ACKNOWLEDGEMENT

The author is extremely thankful to the valued contributors of Facts and Figures on Big Data without which the project could not have been succeeded.

From the author

Over recent times, it is hard to visit a web site, open a newspaper, or read a magazine that does not refer to Big Data. In fact many executives agree to the statement *"if we could harness all of our data, we would be a much stronger business."* The eye-grabbing headline of an October 2012 article in the Harvard Business Review called the data science profession the "Sexiest Job of the 21st Century". Big Data is the result of practically everything in the world being monitored and measured; creating data faster than the available technologies can store, process or manage it. Presently, there has been a surge of unstructured data that requires attention for management. Big Data results in three basic challenges: storing, processing and managing it efficiently. Big Data is one of those mega trends that will impact everyone in one way or another.

This book entitled *'Surprising Mind Blowing Facts and Figures of Big Data'* presents some up-to-date statistics right from evolution to present scenario of how big data is used today and how it is likely affect our lives in the days to come. It also covers forty definitions by thought leaders, tools, platforms, advantages and benefits etc highlighted as follows

- Ø   Sources of Generation of Big Data
- Ø   40 Definitions of Big Data by Thought Leaders
- Ø   Surprising Statistics about Big Data
- Ø   A Comprehensive List of Big Data Statistics
- Ø   17 Big Data and Analytics Developments
- Ø   15 Important Big Data Facts for IT Professionals
- Ø   Big Data in Today's Business and Technology Environment
- Ø   The Market and the Marketers' Challenge with Big Data
- Ø   10 Powerful Facts about Big Data
- Ø   20 Shocking Facts and Figures about "Big Data

- Ø Turning Big Data into Major Insight
- Ø 25 Eye-Opening Facts of Big Data Everyone Should Know
- Ø Big Data Analysis Platforms and Tools
- Ø Three big benefits of big data analytics
- Ø 13 New Trends in Big Data and Data Science

Whether we want it or not Big Data is one of those mega trends that will impact everyone in one way or another. *The book being first of its kind is expected to* be very helpful to wide audiences particularly the new comers in the areas those who want to gain basic knowledge and insight about Big Data.

CONTENTS

Chapter 1: EVOLUTION AND BASIC CONCEPT OF BIG DATA

Over recent times, the concepts of "big data" and "big data analytics" have become ubiquitous, it is hard to visit a web site, open a newspaper, or read a magazine that does not refer to one or both of those phrases. Yet the technologies that are incorporated into big data—massive parallelism, huge data volumes, data distribution, high-speed networks, high-performance computing, task and thread management, and data mining and analytics are not new.

Product Description

"Big Data" is a hot topic and getting a lot of media and business attention. Everyone is talking about big data, from the challenges to yearly spending, job creation and even the tools required for big data projects. Many believe big data will help businesses make better decisions. Big Data is the expression of this gigantic mass of information that we are constantly generating at the global level due to the tremendous amount of data generated daily from fields such as business, research, and sciences. Big Data is everywhere and represents huge opportunities to those who can use it effectively. Big Data is the result of practically everything in the world being monitored and measured; creating data faster than the available technologies can store, process or manage it. Big data is a buzzword that is ambiguous and often misunderstood. But it also feels like it could be the next big thing. Advances in sensing technologies, the digitization of commerce and communications, and the advent and growth in social media are a few of the trends which have created the opportunity to use large scale, fine grained data to understand systems, behavior and commerce; while innovation in technology makes it viable economically to use that information to inform decisions and improve outcomes. Our world is bursting with information, yet we have a lack of data where we need it most: in and about the poorest and most marginalized communities. Therefore, the theme chosen for this year's World Statistics Day, "Better Data for Better Lives". It is realized that high quality statistics are essential for designing and targeting policies to reduce hunger, malnutrition, and rural poverty, and to promote the sustainable use of natural resources for cost effective output. They provide the foundation for evidence-based decision-making for governments and the international community, and play a critical role in measuring and monitoring progress toward national and international development goals and targets. Big data is at the intersection of collecting, organizing, storing, and turning all of that raw data into truly meaningful information. Now the buzzword "big data" refers to the new data-driven paradigm of business, science and technology, where the huge data size and scope enables better and new services, products, and platforms. There are some things that are so big that they have implications for everyone's life, whether we want it or not. Big Data is one of those mega trends that will impact everyone in one way or another. This book entitled 'Surprising Mind Blowing Facts and Figures of Big Data' presents some real-life up-to-date statistics right from evolution to present scenario of how big data is used today and how it is likely affect our lives in the days to come. It also covers forty definitions by thought leaders, tools, Platforms, advantages and benefits. The book being first of its kind is expected to be very useful to wide audiences of students, professionals, decision-makers, and consultants involved in analytics particularly the new comers in the areas those who want to gain basic knowledge about Big Data.

Information has very limited value unless it can take its place within our general understanding of the world. When a financial analyst learns that the price of a stock has suddenly dropped, he cannot help but wonder if the drop of a single stock reflects conditions in other stocks in the same industry. If so, the analyst may check to ensure that other industries are following a downward trend. He may wonder whether the downward trend represents a shift in the national or global economies. Answering the basic question "How does this thing relate to that thing?" is often the central goal of a scientific effort. Ontology are formal systems that relate different information objects into classes and relate classes of information objects to other classes, often as a hierarchical lineage (i.e., classes have super classes and subclasses). Scientific analyses of large information resources can be greatly enhanced if every data object in the resource is positioned somewhere within a formal ontology. Scientists can determine whether observations on a single object will apply to other objects in the same class. Similarly, scientists can begin to ask whether observations that hold true for a class of objects will relate to other classes of objects. Basically, ontology can help scientists do one of their most important tasks—determining how things relate to each other. This chapter will describe how ontology is constructed and how they are used for scientific discovery in Big Data resources.

Big Data resources are highly complex; their data cannot be organized as a simple array of rows and columns. Consequently, the data in Big Data resources must be annotated with information that describes the contained data. The most practical way of associating an object with the data that describe the object is through encapsulation, wherein each data object carries all the information necessary to describe itself. The ability to interrogate a data object for its encapsulated information is called introspection. Introspection is one of the most important features in a well-designed Big Data resource. Without introspection it is difficult, or impossible, to determine whether the data extracted from a query is relevant (has a set of properties that conform to the intended purpose of the query), complete (when combined, represent all of the data in the Big Data resource that is relevant to the query), and meaningful (represent unique, identified data objects, with well-described data values).

It is often assumed that Big Data resources are too large and complex for human comprehension. The analysis of Big Data is best left to software programs. Not so. When data analysts go straight to the complex calculations, before they perform a simple estimation, they will find themselves accepting wildly ridiculous calculations. For comparison purposes, there is nothing quite like a simple and intuitive estimate to pull an overly eager analyst back to reality. Often, the simple act of looking at a stripped-down version of the problem opens a new approach that can drastically reduce computation time. In some situations, analysts will find that a point is reached when higher refinements in methods yield diminishing returns. When everyone has used their most advanced algorithms to make an accurate prediction, they may find that their best effort offers little improvement over a simple estimator. This chapter reviews simple methods for analyzing complex data.

The primary purpose of this book is to explain the principles upon which serious Big Data resources are built. All of the data held in Big Data resources must have a form that supports search, retrieval, and analysis. The analytic methods must be available for review, and the analytic results must be available for validation.

Perhaps the greatest potential benefit of Big Data is the ability to link seemingly disparate disciplines, for the purpose of developing and testing hypotheses that cannot be approached within a single knowledge domain. Methods by which analysts can navigate through different Big Data resources to create new, merged data sets are reviewed.

12 Big Data Definitions

The Berkeley researchers estimated that the world had produced about 1.5 billion gigabytes of information in 1999 and in a 2003 replication of the study (http://www2.sims.berkeley.edu/ research/projects/how-much-info-2003/) found out that amount to have doubled in 3 years. Data was already getting bigger and bigger and around that time, in 2001, industry analyst Doug Laney described the "3Vs"—volume, variety, and velocity as the key "data management challenges" for enterprises, the same "3Vs" that have been used in the last four years by just about anyone attempting to define or describe big data.

The first documented use of the term "big data" appeared in a 1997 paper by scientists at NASA (http://dl.acm.org/citation.cfm?id= 266989.267068&coll=DL&dl=GUIDE), describing the problem they had with visualization (i.e. computer graphics) which "provides an interesting challenge for computer systems: data sets are generally quite large, taxing the capacities of main memory, local disk, and even remote disk. We call this the problem of big data. When data sets do not fit in main memory (in core), or when they do not fit even on local disk, the most common solution is to acquire more resources."

Source: Wikimedia Commons (Fig.-1)

In 2008, a number of prominent American computer scientists popularized the term, predicting that "big-data computing" will "transform the activities of companies, scientific researchers, medical practitioners, and our nation's defense and intelligence operations." The term "big-data computing," however, is never defined in the paper.

The traditional database of authoritative definitions is, of course, the *Oxford English Dictionary* (OED). Here's how the OED defines big data (http://www.forbes.com/fdc/welcome_mjx.shtml).

(Definition #1) "Data of a very large size, typically to the extent that its manipulation and management present significant logistical challenges."

But this is 2014 and maybe the first place to look for definitions should be Wikipedia. Indeed, it looks like the OED followed its lead. Wikipedia defines big data (https://en.wikipedia.org/wiki/Big_data) and it did it before the OED as

(#2) "An all-encompassing term for any collection of data sets so large and complex that it becomes difficult to process using on-hand data management tools or traditional data processing applications."

While a variation of this definition is what is used by most commentators on big data, its similarity to the 1997 definition by the NASA researchers reveals its weakness. "Large" and "traditional" are relative and ambiguous (and potentially self-serving for IT vendors selling either "more resources" of the "traditional" variety or new, non-"traditional" technologies).

The widely-quoted 2011 big data study (http://www.mckinsey.com/insights/business_technology/big_data_the_next_frontier_for_innovation) by McKinsey highlighted that definitional challenge. Defining big data as

(#3) "Datasets whose size is beyond the ability of typical database software tools to capture, store, manage, and analyze," the McKinsey researchers acknowledged that "this definition is intentionally subjective and incorporates a moving definition of how big a dataset needs to be in order to be considered big data." As a result, all the quantitative insights of the study, including the updating of the UC Berkeley numbers by estimating how much new data is stored by enterprises and consumers annually, relate to digital data, rather than just big data, e.g., no attempt was made to estimate how much of the data (or "datasets") enterprises store is big data.

Another prominent source on big data is Viktor Mayer-Schönberger and Kenneth Cukier's book (http://www.forbes.com/fdc/welcome_mjx.shtml) on the subject. Noting that "there is no rigorous definition of big data," they offer one that points to what can be done with the data and why its size matters:

(#4) "The ability of society to harness information in novel ways to produce useful insights or goods and services of significant value" and "…things one can do at a large scale that cannot be done at a smaller one, to extract new insights or create new forms of value."

In *Big   Data@Work*   (http://www.forbes.com/fdc/welcome_ mjx.shtml), Tom Davenport concludes that because of "the problems with the definition" of big data, "I (and other experts I have consulted) predict a relatively short life span for this unfortunate term." Still, Davenport offers this definition:

(#5) "The broad range of new and massive data types that appeared over the last decade or so"

Let me offer a few other possible definitions:

(#6) The new tools helping us find relevant data and analyze its implications.

(#7) The convergence of enterprise and consumer IT

(#8) The shift (for enterprises) from processing internal data to mining external data

(#9) The shift (for individuals) from consuming data to creating data

(#10) The merger of Madame Olympe Maxime and Lieutenant Commander Data

(#11) The belief that the more data you have the more insights and answers will rise automatically from the pool of ones and zeros.

(#12) A new attitude by businesses, non-profits, government agencies, and individuals that combining data from multiple sources could lead to better decisions.

(http://datascience.berkeley.edu/what-is-big-data/) for the compilation of big data definitions from 40+ thought leaders(September 3rd, 2014 by *Jenna Dutcher*; *Big Data* (*datascience@berkeley*)

Sources of Generation of Big Data

There is no single agreed definition of big data. For one, it is data generated through our increasing use of digital devices and web-supported tools and platforms in our daily lives. In any given minute, hundreds of millions of individuals across the globe use some of the world's seven to eight billion mobile phones to make a call send a text message or an email. Or they may wire money, buy a book, search online, pay for a meal with a credit card, update their Face book status, send tweets, upload videos to YouTube, publish a blog post and so on. Each of these actions leaves a digital trace. Added up, this digital information makes up the bulk of big data. Each year since 2012, well over 1.2 zettabytes of data has been produced — 10^{21} bytes, enough to fill 80 billion 16GB iPhones (which would circle the earth more than 100 times - Table 1) And the volume of these data is growing fast. So volume, velocity and variety are the three 'Vs' that characterize big data, with the value that could be extracted from them often added as a fourth V

Table 1— Data 'inflation'

Unit	Size	What it means
Bit (b)	1 or 0	Short for "binary digit", after the binary code (1 or 0) computers use to store and process data— including text, numbers, images, videos, etc.
Byte (B)	8 bits	Enough information to create a number or an English letter in computer code. It is the basic unit of computing.
Kilobyte (KB)	1,000, or 2^{10}, bytes	From "thousand" in Greek. One page of typed text is 2KB.
Megabyte	1,000KB,	From "large" in Greek. The MP3 file of a typical

Unit	Size	What it means
(MB)	or 2^{20}, bytes	song is about 4MB.
Gigabytes (GB)	1,000MB, or 2^{30}, bytes	From "giant" in Greek. A two-hour film can be compressed into 1-2GB. A 1GB text file contains over 1 billion characters, or roughly 290 copies of Shakespeare's complete works.
Terabyte (TB)	1,000GB, or 2^{40}, bytes	From "monster" in Greek. All the catalogued books in America's Library of Congress total 15TB. All the tweets sent before the end of 2013 would approximately fill an 18.5TB text file. Printing such a file (at a rate of 15 A4-sized pages per minute) would take over 1200 years.
Petabyte (PB)	1,000TB, or 2^{50}, bytes	The NSA is reportedly analyzing 1.6 per cent of global Internet traffic, or about 30PB, per day. Continuously playing 30PB of music would take over 60,000 years, which corresponds to the time that has elapsed since the first *Homo Sapiens* left Africa.
Exabyte (EB)	1,000PB, or 2^{60}, bytes	1EB of data corresponds to the storage capacity of 33,554,432 iPhone 5 devices with a 32GB memory. By 2018, the total volume of monthly mobile data traffic is forecast to be about half of an EB. If this volume of data were stored on 32GB iPhone 5 devices stacked one on top of the other, the pile would be over 283 times the height of the Empire State Building.
Zettabyte (ZB)	1,000EB, or 2^{70}, bytes	It is estimated that in 2013, humanity generated 4-5ZB of data, which exceeds the quantity of data in 46 trillion print issues of *The Economist*. If that many magazines were laid out sheet by

Unit	Size	What it means
		sheet on the ground, they would cover the total land surface area of the Earth.
Yottabyte (YB)	1,000ZB, or 2^{80}, bytes	The contents of one human's genetic code can be stored in less than 1.5GB, meaning that 1YB of storage could contain the genome of over 800 trillion people, or roughly that of 100,000 times the entire world population.

The prefixes are set by the International Bureau of Weights and Measures. Source: Adapted and updated from The Economist by Emmanuel Letouzé and Gabriel Pestre, using data from Cisco, the Daily Mail, Twitter (via quora.com*), SEC Archives (via* expandedramblings.com*),* Bitesizebio.com*, and the book Uncharted: Big Data as a Lens on Human Culture (2013) by Erez Aiden and Jean-Baptiste Michel.*

And much as a population with a sudden outburst of fertility gets both larger and younger, the proportion of digital data produced recently is growing ever faster — up to 90 per cent of the world's data was created over just two years (2010–2012), according to one much cited account.

Types of Data

Big data come in different types. ***One kind*** is small pieces of 'hard' data — numbers or facts, for example — described by Alex 'Sandy' pent land, a professor at the Massachusetts Institute of Technology, United States, as "digital breadcrumbs". They are said to be 'structured' because they make up datasets of variables that can be easily tagged, categorized, and organized (in columns and rows for instance) for systematic analysis. One example is Call Detail Records (CDRs) collected by mobile phone operators (Table 2). CDRs are metadata (data about data) that capture subscribers' use of their cellphones — including an identification code and, at a minimum, the location of the phone tower that routed the call for both caller and receiver — and the time and duration of call. Large operators collect over six billion CDRs per day (Figure 2).

Table 2—Data contained in a CDR

Variable	Data
Caller ID	X76VG588RLPQ
Caller ID tower location	2°24' 22.14" , 35°49' 56.54
Recipient phone number	A81UTC93KK52A81UTC93KK52
Recipient cell tower location	3°26' 30.47", 31°12' 18:01"
Call time	3013-11-07T15:15:00
Call duration	01:12:02

Note: only the phone tower location is given for privacy reason.
Source: New primer on mobile phone network data for development
(http://www.unglobalpulse.org/Mobile_Phone_Network_Data-for-Dev).
(UN Global Pulse, 5 November 2013)

A second kind of big data are videos, documents, blog posts and other social media content. Most of these data are 'unstructured' — and so harder to analyze. They differ from 'breadcrumbs' in that they are subject to their authors' editorial choices and, being subjective, may paint a deceiving picture. For example, you might blog that you are boycotting a certain product, but your credit card statement may reveal a different preference based on actual purchases.

A third kind of big data is gathered remotely by digital sensors and reflects human actions. These might be 'smart meters' installed in homes to record electricity consumption, or satellite imagery that can pick up physical information such as vegetation cover as an indicator of deforestation.

Some consider the universe of big data to be much wider including administrative records, price or weather data, for instance, or books that have been previously digitized which, taken collectively, may **constitute a fourth kind**.

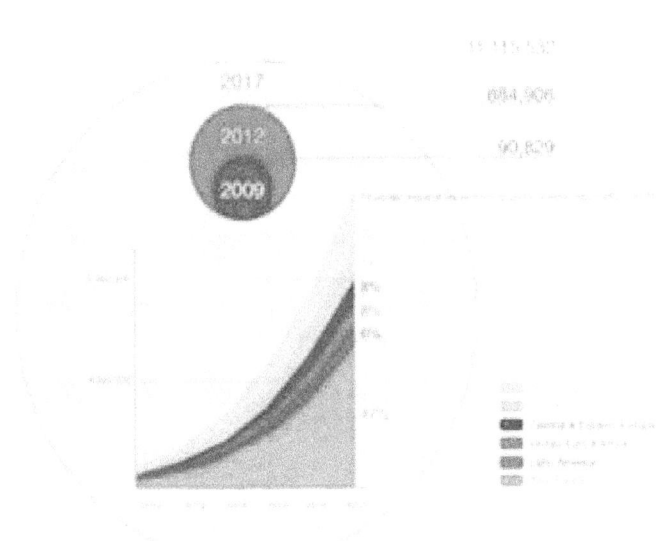

Figure 2: Global Mobile Data 2014 - Traffic growth and forecast

How big will Big Data get?

The digital universe will grow from 3.2 zettabytes today to 40 zettabytes in only six years (One zettabyte is roughly a billion terabytes). "When we look at the data volumes coming at us, it's *mind-*

blowing," said Horton works CEO Rob Bearden in his keynote address at Hadoop Summit 2014 in San Jose, Calif. "The data volume in the enterprise is going to grow 50x year-over-year between now and 2020. I think the most important thing to recognize is that 85% of that data is coming from net-new data sources." And these sources, including *mobile, social media, and web and machine-generated data,* present both a challenge and an opportunity for enterprises globally, Bearden noted (Source: Hadoop Summit 2014).

More than a buzzword big data, however you define it, has been praised and vilified. Its many things too many people: a boon to scientists (http://www.informationweek.com/big-data/hardware-architectures/how-nasa-manages-big-data-/d/d-id/899791) and retailers, but also an enabling technology for a host of privacy and security threats   (http://www.informationweek.com/big-data/big-data-analytics/white-house-big-data-report-5-privacy-takeaways/d/d-id/1235054).

Source: (http://datascience.berkeley.edu/feed/)

What do we mean by Big Data?

The term "Big Data" has come into vogue to refer not just to data volume, but also to for an exciting new set of applications and techniques that are powering modern applications and whose novelty seems to be changing the way the world is computing. In most cases, the "end game" is the application of well-known statistical and machine-learning techniques. However, modern distributed computation techniques are allowing the analysis of data sets far larger than those that could be typically analyzed in the past.

Many organizations can find the massive amounts of data generated from high-volume transactions, call centers, sensors, web logs, and digital images overwhelming. The success of your business depends on meeting big data challenges, while continually improving operational efficiency. Whether you are facing demands for faster analytics, more transactions or uninterrupted availability, your data systems must be flexible and resilient to address these challenges. Having a robust data system is fundamental. More importantly, different data workloads require specialized capabilities to excel.

Back in the day, when technology wasn't very advanced, almost every business leader relied on basic scientific studies and statistics to predict trends about consumer behavior. However, Internet has gained traction, and business has become more and more global. Every day, wealth of information is derived from social media, and mobile phones. Data has begun to surge and enter the business lexicon. It was, therefore, important for every business leader to keep pace with new technology and understand the importance of the new medium, Big Data. To keep a track on Terabytes, Petabytes, Exabytes of data, and ascertain predictive information, Data Scientists are winning favor from the best employers of the world.

According to Gartner (http://www.gartner.com/technology/home.jsp), information becomes big data when the volume can no longer be managed with normal database tools. Due to the mountain of information that companies are producing and spreading through social networks, CIOs are now facing the challenge of processing all this data in a short time.

In recent years, the volume of data produced by users has risen inexorably, particularly with the emergence of new sources such as social networks, connected TVs, Smart phones and touch-screen tablets, etc. Anyone can now create content in real time and share it via his or her favourite channels. Companies keep producing and storing ever-increasing amounts of data, resulting in the ***saturation of their databases.***

Big Data is the expression of this gigantic mass of information that we are constantly generating at the global level.

The 3 Vs of Big Data

Big Data cannot just be reduced to a problem caused by the sheer amount of data. The most comprehensive definition of the phenomenon is summarized in three points known as the "3Vs" of Big Data: **Volume, Variety and Velocity**

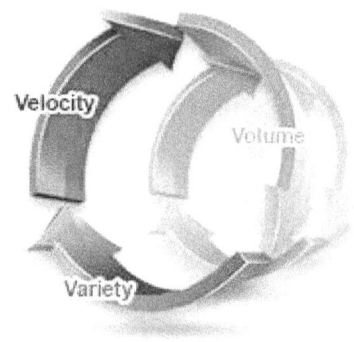

Figure 3: Volume, Variety and Velocity

- **Volume:** Companies must understand this growing volume of data and find ways of storing and processing this deluge of terabytes or even petabytes of data.
- **Variety:** Big Data encompasses both structured and unstructured data originating originate from an increasingly diverse range of sources (mobile equipment, images, videos, audio, geo-location, social networks, etc.).
- **Velocity:** The amount of data is increasing, but they need to be processed just as quickly, or even in real time. Big Data

solutions must allow for the exploitation of this data before it loses its value.

Big Data thus requires the creation of new architectures to overcome the limitations of current BI systems and satisfy the requirements of the three Vs. These architectures must be capable of **capturing, storing, processing and analyzing** this amount of data in a new way in order to optimize these data and meet these new needs *(Source:http://www.ingensi.com/en/le-big-data/en-chiffres-big-data)*

Definitions of Big Data by Thought Leaders / Experts

What is Big Data? **"Big data" It seems like the phrase is everywhere. The term was added to the Oxford English Dictionary in 2013** (http://mashable.com/2013/06/13/dictionary-new-words-2013/) **and appeared in Merriam-Webster's Collegiate Dictionary in 2014** (http://www.computerworld.com/article/2489571/it-management/selfie--big-data-and---make-the-2014-dictionary.html)**.   Now, Gartner's just-released 2014 Hype Cycle** (http://siliconangle.com/blog/2014/08/19/gartners-hype-cycle-big-datas-on-the-slippery-slope/) **shows "big data" passing the "peak of inflated expectations" and moving on its way down into the "trough of disillusionment." Big data is all the rage. But what does it actually mean?**

A commonly repeated definition (http://www.gartner.com/it-glossary/ big-data/) cites the three Vs: volume, velocity, and variety. But others argue that it's not the size of data (http://datascience.berkeley.edu/ big-data-infographic/) that counts, but the tools being used or the insights that can be drawn from a dataset.

Top recurring themes in our thought leaders' definitions (word cloud via Wordle ⌕)

To settle the question once and for all, we asked more than 40 thought leaders in publishing, fashion, food, automobiles, medicine, marketing, and every industry in between how exactly they would define the phrase "big data." Their answers might surprise you! Take a look below to find out what big data is:

John Akred

Founder and CTO, Silicon Valley Data Science (http://svds.com/) ⌕

"Big Data" refers to a combination of an approach to informing decision making with analytical insight derived from data,

and a set of enabling technologies that enable that insight to be economically derived from at times very large, diverse sources of data. Advances in sensing technologies, the digitization of commerce and communications, and the advent and growth in social media are a few of the trends which have created the opportunity to use large scale, fine grained data to understand systems, behavior and commerce; while innovation in technology makes it viable economically to use that information to inform decisions and improve outcomes.

Philip Ashlock

Chief   Architect, Data.gov   (http://www.data.gov/) ⬀
Twitter: @philipashlock (https://twitter.com/philipashlock) ⬀

While the use of the term is quite nebulous and is often co-opted for other purposes, I've understood "big data" to be about analysis for data that's really messy or where you don't know the right questions or queries to make — analysis that can help you find patterns, anomalies, or new structures amidst otherwise chaotic or complex data points. Usually this revolves around datasets with a byte size that seems fairly large relative to our frame of reference using files on a desktop PC (e.g., larger than a terabyte) and many of the tools around big data are to help deal with a large volume of data, but to me the most important concepts of big data don't actually have much to do with it being "big" in this sense (especially since that's such a relative term these days). In fact, they can often be applied to smaller datasets as well. Natural language processing and lucene based search engines are good examples of big data techniques and tools that are often used with relatively small amounts of data.

Jon Bruner

Editor-at-Large, O'Reilly Media (http://www.oreilly.com/)   ⬀
Twitter: @JonBruner (https://twitter.com/JonBruner) ⬀

Big Data is the result of collecting information at its most granular level — it's what you get when you instrument a system and keep all of the data that your instrumentation is able to gather.

Reid Bryant

Data Scientist, Brooks Bell (http://www.brooksbell.com/) ⌐

As computational efficiency continues to increase, "big data" will be less about the actual size of a particular dataset and more about the specific expertise needed to process it. With that in mind, "big data" will ultimately describe any dataset large enough to necessitate high-level programming skill and statistically defensible methodologies in order to transform the data asset into something of value.

Mike Cavaretta

Data Scientist and Manager, Ford Motor Company (http://www.ford.com/) ⌐ Twitter: @mjcavaretta ⌐

You cannot give me too much data. I see big data as storytelling — whether it is through information graphics or other visual aids that explain it in a way that allows others to understand across sectors. I always push for the full scope of the data over averages and aggregations — and I like to go to the raw data because of the possibilities of things you can do with it.

Drew Conway

Head of Data, Project Florida (http://sum.com/) ⌐ Twitter: @drewconway (https://twitter.com/drewconway) ⌐

Big data, which started as a technological innovation in distributed computing, is now a cultural movement by which we continue to discover how humanity interacts with the world — and each other — at large-scale.

Rohan Deuskar

CEO and Co-Founder, Stylitics (https://www.stylitics.com/) ⬀
Twitter: @RohanD (https://twitter.com/RohanD) ⬀

Big data refers to the approach to data of "collect now, sort out later"…meaning you capture and store data on a very large volume of actions and transactions of different types, on a continuous basis, in order to make sense of it later. The low cost of storage and better methods of analysis mean that you generally don't need to have a specific purpose for the data in mind before you collect it.

Amy Escobar

Data Scientist, 2U, Inc (http://2u.com/) ⬀

[Big data is] an opportunity to gain a more complex understanding of the relationships between different factors and to uncover previously undetected patterns in data by leveraging advances in the technical aspects of collecting, storing, and retrieving data along with innovative ideas and techniques for manipulating and analyzing data.

Josh Ferguson

Chief Technology Officer, Mode Analytics (https://modeanalytics.com/) ⬀

Big data is the broad name given to challenges and opportunities we have as data about every aspect of our lives becomes available. It's not just about data though; it also includes the people, processes, and analysis that turn data into meaning.

John Foreman

Chief Data Scientist, Mail Chimp (http://mailchimp.com/) ⬀
Twitter: @John4man (https://twitter.com/John4man) ⬀

I prefer a flexible but functional definition of big data. Big data is when your business wants to use data to solve a problem, answer a question, produce a product, etc., but the standard, simple methods (maybe it's SQL, maybe it's k-means, maybe it's a single server with a crone job) break down on the size of the data set, causing time, effort, creativity, and money to be spent crafting a solution to the problem that leverages the data without simply sampling or tossing out records.

The main consideration here, then, is to weigh the cost of using "all the data" in this complex (and potentially brittle) solution versus the benefits gained over using a smaller data set in a cheaper, faster, more stable way.

Daniel Gillick

Senior Research Scientist, Google ⤴

Historically, most decisions — political, military, business, and personal — have been made by brains [that] have unpredictable logic and operate on subjective experiential evidence. "Big data" represents a cultural shift in which more and more decisions are made by algorithms with transparent logic, operating on documented immutable evidence. I think "big" refers more to the pervasive nature of this change than to any particular amount of data.

Vincent Granville

Co-Founder, Data   Science   Central (http://www.datasciencecentral.com/) ⤴
Twitter: @AnalyticBridge (https://twitter.com/AnalyticBridge) ⤴

Big data is data that even when efficiently compressed still contains 5-10 times more information (measured in entropy or predictive power, per unit of time) than what you are used to right now. It may require a different approach to extract value.

Annette Greiner

Lecturer, UC   Berkeley   School   of   Information (http://www.ischool.berkeley.edu/) ⬀ Web Application Developer at NERSC, Lawrence Berkeley National Lab Twitter: @annettegreiner (https://twitter.com/annettegreiner) ⬀

Big data is data that contains enough observations to demand unusual handling because of its sheer size, though what are unusual changes over time and varies from one discipline to another. Scientific computing is accustomed to pushing the envelope, constantly developing techniques to address relentless growth in dataset size, but many other disciplines are now just discovering the value — and hence the challenges — of working with data at the unwieldy end of the scale.

Seth Grimes

Principal Consultant, Alta Plana Corporation (http://altaplana. com/sethgrimes.html) ⬀ Twitter: @SethGrimes (https://twitter.com/ SethGrimes) ⬀

Big data has taken a beating in recent years, the accusation being that marketers and analysts have stretched and squeezed the term to cover a multitude of disparate problems, technologies, and products. Yet the core of big data remains what it has been for over a decade, framed by Doug Laney's 2001 three Vs, Volume, Velocity, and Variety, and indicating data challenges sufficient to justify non-routine computing resources and processing techniques.

Joel Gurin

Author of *Open Data Now* (http://www.opendatanow.com/) ⬀ Twitter: @JoelGurin (https://twitter.com/JoelGurin) ⬀

Big data describes datasets that are so large, complex, or rapidly changing that they push the very limits of our analytical capability. It's a subjective term: What seems "big" today may seem modest in a few years when our analytic capacity has improved. While big data can be about anything, the most important kinds of big data — and perhaps the only ones worth the effort — are those that can have a big impact through what they tell us about society, public health, the economy, scientific research, or any number of other large-scale subjects.

Quentin Hardy

Deputy   Tech   Editor, *The   New   York   Times* ⬈
Twitter: @qhardy (https://twitter.com/qhardy) ⬈

What's "big" in big data isn't necessarily the size of the databases, it's the big number of data sources we have, as digital sensors and behavior trackers migrate across the world. As we triangulate information in more ways, we will discover hitherto unknown patterns in nature and society — and pattern-making is the wellspring of new art, science, and commerce.

Harlan Harris

Director, Data Science at Education Advisory Board (https://www.eab.com/) ⬈ President and Co-Founder, Data Community DC (https://www.eab.com/)⬈   Twitter: @HarlanH (https://twitter.com/HarlanH) ⬈

To me, "big data" is the situation where an organization can (arguably) say that they have access to what they need to reconstruct, understand, and model the part of the world that they care about. Using their big data, then, they can (try to) predict future states of the world, optimize their processes, and otherwise be more effective and rational in their activities.

Jessica Kirkpatrick

Director of Data Science, Insta EDU (https://instaedu.com/tutors/) ⬀ Twitter: @berkeleyjess (https://twitter.com/berkeleyjess) ⬀

Big data refers to using complex datasets to drive focus, direction, and decision making within a company or organization. This is done by deriving actionable insights from the analysis of your organization's data.

David Leonhardt

Editor, The Upshot (http://www.nytimes.com/upshot/?_r=2) ⬀ *The New York Times* Twitter: @DLeonhardt (https://twitter.com/DLeonhardt) ⬀

Big Data is nothing more than a tool for capturing reality — just as newspaper reporting, photography and long-form journalism are. But it's an exciting tool, because it holds the potential of capturing reality in some clearer and more accurate ways than we have been able to do in the past.

Hilary Mason

Founder, Fast Forward Labs (http://www.fastforwardlabs.com/) ⬀ Twitter: @hmason (https://twitter.com/hmason) ⬀

Big data is just the ability to gather information and query it in such a way that we are able to learn things about the world that were previously inaccessible to us.

Deirdre Mulligan

Associate Professor, UC Berkeley School of Information (http://www.ischool.berkeley.edu/) ⬀

Big data: Endless possibilities or cradle-to-grave shackles, depending upon the political, ethical, and legal choices we make.

Sharmila Mulligan

CEO and Founder, ClearStory Data (http://www.clearstorydata.com/) ⌕   Twitter: @ShahaniMulligan   (https://twitter.com/ShahaniMulligan) ⌕

[Big data means] harnessing more sources of diverse data where "data variety" and "data velocity" are the key opportunities. (Each source represents "a signal" on what is happening in the business.) The opportunity is to harness data variety [and] automate "harmonization" of data sources to deliver fast-updating insights consumable by the line-of-business users.

Sean Patrick Murphy

Consulting Data Scientist and Co-Founder of a stealth startup Twitter: @sayhitosean (https://twitter.com/sayhitosean) ⌕

While "big data" is often large in size relative to the available tool set, "big" actually refers to being important. Scientists and engineers have long known that data is valuable, but now the rest of the world, including those in control of purse strings, understand the value that can be created from data.

Prakash Nanduri

Co-Founder,   CEO   and   President, Paxata,   Inc (http://www.paxata.com/) ⌕

Everything we know spits out data today — not just the devices we use for computing. We now get digital exhaust from our garage door openers to our coffee pots, and everything in between. At the same time, we have become a generation of people who demand instantaneous access to information — from what the weather is like in a country thousands of miles away to which store has better deals on toaster ovens. Big data is at the intersection of collecting, organizing, storing, and turning all of that raw data into truly meaningful information.

Chris Neumann

CEO and Co-Founder, Data Hero (https://datahero.com/) ⤤ Twitter: @ckneumann (https://twitter.com/ckneumann) ⤤

At Aster Data, we originally used the term big data in our marketing to refer to analytical MPP databases like ours and to differentiate them from traditional data warehouse software. While both were capable of storing a "big" volume of data (which, in 2008, we defined as 10 TB or greater), "big data" systems were capable of performing complex analytics on top of that data — something that legacy data warehouse software could not do. Thus, our original definition was a system that (1) was capable of storing 10 TB of data or more and (2) was capable of executing advanced workloads, such as behavioral analytics or market basket analysis, on those large volumes of data. As time went on, diversity of data started to become more prevalent in these systems (particularly the need to mix structured and unstructured data), which led to more widespread adoption of the "3 Vs" (volume, velocity, and variety) as a definition for big data, which continues to this day.

Cathy O'Neil

Program Director, the Lede Program (http://www.journalism.columbia.edu/page/1058-the-lede-program-an-introduction-to-data-practices/906) ⤤ at Columbia University Twitter: @mathbabedotorg (https://twitter.com/mathbabedotorg) ⤤

"Big data" is more than one thing, but an important aspect is its use as a rhetorical device, something that can be used to deceive or mislead or overhype. It is thus vitally important that people who deploy big data models consider not just technical issues but the ethical issues as well.

Brad Peters

Chief   Product   Officer,   Chairman   at Birst (https://www.birst.com/) ⌐

*In my view, **big data is data that requires novel processing techniques to handle.** Typically, big data requires massive parallelism in some fashion (storage and/or compute) to deal with volume and processing variety.*

Gregory Piatetsky-Shapiro

President   and   Editor1, KDnuggets.com (http://www.kdnuggets.com/) ⌐
Twitter: @kdnuggets (https://twitter.com/kdnuggets) ⌐

*The best definition I saw is, "Data is big when data size becomes part of the problem." However, this refers to the size only. **Now the buzzword "big data" refers to the new data-driven paradigm of business, science and technology, where the huge data size and scope enables better and new services, products, and platforms.** # Big Data also generates a lot of hype and will probably be replaced by a new buzzword, like "Internet of Things," but "big data"-enabled services companies, like Google, Face book, Amazon, location services, personalized/precision medicine, and many more will remain and prosper.*

Jake Porway

Founder   and   Executive   Director, Data   Kind (http://www.datakind.org/) ⌐Twitter: @DataKind (https://twitter.com/ DataKind) ⌐, @jakeporway (https://twitter.com/jakeporway) ⌐

*As our lives have moved from the physical to the digital world, our everyday tools like smart phones and ubiquitous Internet create vast amounts of data. **One of the best interpretations of the "big" in*** *"big data" is expansive — whether you are a Fortune 500 company who just released an app that is creating a torrent of user data about every click and every activity of every user or a nonprofit who just launched a cell phone based app to find the closest homeless shelters that are now spewing forth information about every search and every click, we all have data. Dealing with this so-called big data requires a massive shift in technologies for storing, processing, and managing data — but also presents tremendous opportunity for the social sector to gather and analyze information faster to address some of our world's most pressing challenges.*

Kyle Rush

Head of Optimization, Optimizely (https://www.optimizely.com/) ⏷
Twitter: @kylerush (https://twitter.com/kylerush) ⏷

There is certainly a colorful variety of definitions for the term big data out there. To me it means working with data at a large scale and velocity.

AnnaLee Saxenian

Dean, UC Berkeley School of Information (http://www.ischool.berkeley.edu/) ⏷   Twitter: @annosax (https://twitter.com/annosax) ⏷

I'm not fond of the phrase "big data" because it focuses on the volume of data, obscuring the far-reaching changes are making data essential to individuals and organizations in today's world. But if I have to define it I'd say that "big data" is data that can't be processed using standard databases because it is too big, too fast-moving, or too complex for traditional data processing tools.

Josh Schwartz

Chief Data Scientist, Chartbeat (https://chartbeat.com/) ⏷
Twitter: @joshuadschwartz (https://twitter.com/joshuadschwartz) ⏷

The rising accessibility of platforms for the storage and analysis of large amounts of data (and the falling price per TB of doing so) has made it possible for a wide variety of organizations to store nearly all data in their purview — every log line, customer interaction, and event — un-aggregated and for a significant period of time. The associated ethos of "store everything now and ask questions later" to me more than anything else characterizes how the world of computational systems looks under the lens of modern "big data" systems.

Peter Skomoroch

Entrepreneur, former Principal Data Scientist, LinkedIn (https://www.linkedin.com/nhome/) ☐ʼ   Twitter: @peteskomoroch (https://twitter.com/peteskomoroch) ☐ʼ

Big data originally described the practice in the consumer Internet industry of applying algorithms to increasingly large amounts of disparate data to solve problems that had suboptimal solutions with smaller datasets. Many features and signals can only be observed by collecting massive amounts of data (for example, the relationships across an entire social network), and would not be detected using smaller samples. Processing large datasets in this manner was often difficult, time consuming, and error prone before the advent of technologies like MapReduce and Hadoop, which ushered in a wave of related tools and applications now collectively called big data technologies.

Anna Smith

Analytics Engineer, Rent the Runway (https://www.renttherunway.com/) ☐ʼ   Twitter: @OMGannaks (https://twitter.com/OMGannaks) ☐ʼ

Big data is when data grows to the point that the technology supporting the data has to change. It also encompasses a variety of topics relating to how disparate data can be combined, processed into insights, and/or reworked into smart products.

Ryan Swanstrom

Data Science Blogger, Data Science 101 (http://101.datascience.community/) ⤤ Twitter: @swgoof (https://twitter.com/swgoof) ⤤

Big data used to mean data that a single machine was unable to handle. Now big data has become a buzzword to mean anything related to data analytics or visualization.

Shashi Upadhyay

CEO and Founder, Lattice Engines (http://www.lattice-engines.com/) ⤤
Twitter: @shashiSF (https://twitter.com/shashiSF) ⤤

Big data is an umbrella term that means a lot of different things, but to me, it means the possibility of doing extraordinary things using modern machine learning techniques on digital data. Whether it is predicting illness, the weather, the spread of infectious diseases, or what you will buy next, it offers a world of possibilities for improving people's lives.

Mark van Rijmenam

CEO/Founder, BigData-Startups (http://bigdata-startups.com/) ⤤
Author of Think Bigger (http://www.amazon.com/gp/product/ 0814434150) ⤤ Twitter: @VanRijmenam (https://twitter.com/ VanRijmenam) ⤤

Big data is not all about volume; it is more about combining different data sets and to analyze it in real-time to get insights for your organization. Therefore, the right definition of big data should in fact be: mixed data.

Hal Varian

Chief   Economist, Google ⟂   Twitter: @halvarian (https://twitter.com/halvarian) ⟂

Big data means data that cannot fit easily into a standard relational database.

Timothy Weaver

CIO, Del   Monte   Foods   (http://www.delmonte.com/) ⟂ Twitter: @DelMonteCIO (https://twitter.com/DelMonteCIO) ⟂

I'm happy to repeat the definition I've heard used and think appropriately defines the over [all] subject. I believe its Forrester's definition of Volume, Velocity, Variety, and Variability. A lot of different data is coming fast and in different structures.

Steven Weber

Professor, UC   Berkeley   School   of   Information (http://www.ischool.berkeley.edu/) ⟂ and Department of Political Science

For me, the technological definitions (like "too big to fit in an Excel spreadsheet" or "too big to hold in memory") are important, but aren't really the main point. Big data for me is data at a scale and scope that changes in some fundamental way (not just at margins) the range of solutions that can be considered when people and organizations face a complex problem. Different solutions, not just 'more, better.'

John Myles White

Twitter: @johnmyleswhite (https://twitter.com/johnmyleswhite) ⟂

The term big data is really only useful if it describes a quantity of data that's so large that traditional approaches to data analysis are

doomed to failure. That can mean that you're doing complex analytics on data that's too large to fit into memory or it can mean that you're dealing with a data storage system that doesn't offer the full functionality of a standard relational database. What's essential is that your old way of doing things doesn't apply anymore and can't just be scaled out.

Brian Wilt

Senior Data Scientist, Jawbone (https://jawbone.com/) ⤢
Twitter: @brianwilt (https://twitter.com/brianwilt) ⤢

*The joke is that **big data is data that breaks Excel**, but we try not to be snooty about whether you measure your data in MBs or PBs. Data is more about your team and the results they can get.*

Raymond Yee, Ph.D.

Software Developer, unglue.it (https://unglue.it/) ⤢
Twitter: @rdhyee (https://twitter.com/rdhyee) ⤢

Big data enchants us with the promise of new insights. Let's not forget the knowledge hidden in the small data right before us.

Big Data versus Small Data

What exactly is Big Data? Big Data can be characterized by the three V's: volume (large amounts of data), variety (includes different types of data), and velocity (constantly accumulating new data). Those of us who have worked on Big Data projects might suggest throwing a few more V's into the mix: vision (having a purpose and a plan), verification (ensuring that the data conforms to a set of specifications), and validation (checking that its purpose is fulfilled) (http://www.sciencedirect.com/science/article/pii/B9780124045767099 822#ge0695).

Big Data is not small data that has become bloated to the point that it can no longer fit on a spreadsheet, nor is it a database that happens to be very large. Nonetheless, some professionals who customarily work with relatively small data sets harbor the false impression that they can apply their spreadsheet and database skills directly to Big Data resources without mastering new skills and without adjusting to new analytic paradigms. As they see things, when the data gets bigger, only the computer must adjust (by getting faster, acquiring more volatile memory, and increasing its storage capabilities); Big Data poses no special problems that a supercomputer could not solve.

This attitude, which seems to be prevalent among database managers, programmers, and statisticians, is highly counterproductive. It leads to slow and ineffective software, huge investment losses, bad analyses, and the production of useless and irreversibly defective Big Data resources.

Let us look at a few of the general differences that can help distinguish Big Data and small data.

1. Goals

Small data—usually designed to answer a specific question or serve a particular goal.

Big Data—usually designed with a goal in mind, but the goal is flexible and the questions posed are protean. Here is a short, imaginary funding announcement for Big Data grants designed "to combine high-quality data from fisheries, Coast Guard, commercial shipping, and coastal management agencies for a growing data collection that can be used to support a variety of governmental and commercial management studies in the Lower Peninsula." In this fictitious case, there is a vague goal, but it is obvious that there really is no way to completely specify what the Big Data resource will contain and how the various types of data held in the resource will be organized, connected to other data resources, or usefully analyzed. Nobody can specify, with any degree of confidence, the ultimate destiny of any Big Data project; it usually comes as a surprise.

2. Location

Small data—typically, small data is contained within one institution, often on one computer, sometimes in one file.

Big Data—typically spread throughout electronic space, typically parceled onto multiple Internet servers, located anywhere on earth.

3. Data structure and content

Small data—ordinarily contains highly structured data. The data domain is restricted to a single discipline or sub-discipline. The data often comes in the form of uniform records in an ordered spreadsheet.

Big Data—Must be capable of absorbing unstructured data (e.g., such as free-text documents, images, motion pictures, sound recordings, physical objects). The subject matter of the resource may cross multiple disciplines, and the individual data objects in the resource may link to data contained in other, seemingly unrelated, Big Data resources.

4. Data preparation

Small data—in many cases, the data user prepares her own data, for her own purposes.

Big Data—the data comes from many diverse sources, and it is prepared by many people. People who use the data are seldom the people who have prepared the data.

5. Longevity

Small data—when the data project ends, the data is kept for a limited time (seldom longer than 7 years, the traditional academic life span for research data) and then is discarded.

Big Data—Big Data projects typically contain data that must be stored in perpetuity. Ideally, data stored in a Big Data resource will be absorbed into another resource when the original resource terminates. Many Big Data projects extend into the future and the past (e.g., legacy data), accruing data prospectively and retrospectively.

6. Measurements

Small data—typically, the data is measured using one experimental protocol, and the data can be represented using one set of standard units (see Glossary item, Protocol).

Big Data—many different types of data are delivered in many different electronic formats. Measurements, when present, may be obtained by many different protocols. Verifying the quality of Big Data is one of the most difficult tasks for data managers.

7. Reproducibility

Small data—Projects are typically repeatable. If there is some question about the quality of the data, reproducibility of the data, or validity of the conclusions drawn from the data, the entire project can be repeated, yielding a new data set.

Big Data—Replication of a Big Data project is seldom feasible. In most instances, all that anyone can hope for is that bad data in a Big Data resource will be found and flagged as such.

8. Stakes

Small data—Project costs are limited. Laboratories and institutions can usually recover from the occasional small data failure.

Big Data—Big Data projects can be obscenely expensive. A failed Big Data effort can lead to bankruptcy, institutional collapse, mass firings, and the sudden disintegration of all the data held in the resource. As an example, an NIH Big Data project known as the "NCI cancer Biomedical Informatics Grid" cost at least $350 million for fiscal years 2004 to 2010 (see Glossary item, Grid). An ad hoc committee reviewing the resource found that despite the intense efforts of hundreds of cancer researchers and information specialists, it had accomplished so little and at so great an expense that a project moratorium was called.[3] Soon thereafter, the resource was terminated.[4] Though the costs of failure can be high in terms of money, time, and labor, Big Data failures may have some redeeming value. Each failed effort lives on as intellectual remnants consumed by the next Big Data effort.

9. Introspection

Small data—Individual data points are identified by their row and column location within a spreadsheet or database table (see Glossary item, Data point). If you know the row and column headers, you can find and specify all of the data points contained within.

Big Data—unless the Big Data resource is exceptionally well designed, the contents and organization of the resource can be inscrutable, even to the data managers (see Glossary item, Data manager). Complete access to data, information about the data values, and information about the organization of the data is achieved through a technique herein referred to as introspection (see Glossary item, Introspection).

10. Analysis

Small data—in most instances, all of the data contained in the data project can be analyzed together, and all at once.

Big Data—With few exceptions, such as those conducted on supercomputers or in parallel on multiple computers, Big Data is ordinarily analyzed in incremental steps (see Glossary items, Parallel computing, Map Reduce). The data are extracted, reviewed, reduced, normalized, transformed, visualized, interpreted, and reanalyzed with different methods.

The Most Common Purpose of Big Data is to Produce Small Data

Big Data is seldom, if ever, analyzed in Toto. There is almost always a drastic filtering process that reduces Big Data into smaller data. This rule applies to scientific analyses. *The Australian Square Kilometer Array of radio telescopes, World Wide Telescope, CERN's Large Hadron Collider, and the Panoramic Survey Telescope and Rapid Response System array of telescopes produce petabytes of data every day* (see Glossary items, Square Kilometer Array, Large Hadron Collider, World Wide Telescope). Researchers use these raw data sources to produce much smaller data sets for analysis.

Here is an example showing how workable subsets of data are prepared from Big Data resources. *Blazers are rare super-massive black holes that release jets of energy moving at near-light speeds. Cosmologists want to know as much as they can about these strange objects. A first step to studying blazers is to locate as many of these objects as possible. Afterward, various measurements on all of the collected blazers can be compared and their general characteristics can be determined. Blazers seem to have a gamma ray signature not present in other celestial objects.* The Wide-field Infrared Survey Explorer (WISE) collected infrared data on the entire observable universe. Researchers extracted from the WISE data every celestial body associated with an infrared signature in the gamma ray range that was suggestive of blazers about 300 objects. Further research on these 300 objects led researchers to believe that about half were blazers (about 150). This is how Big Data research typically works—by constructing small data sets that can be productively analyzed.

The chapter is nontechnical all dealing in one way or another with the consequences of our exploitation of Big Data resources. These chapters cover knowledge about legal, social, and ethical issues. The book ends with predictions for the future of Big Data and its impending impact on the world. The book is prepared keeping in view of vast array of inquisitive minds eager to know about big data particularly those readers unfamiliar with technical language and concepts about big data. Readers with a strong informatics background may enjoy the book more with up-to-date statistics presented in this book.

Readers may notice that many of the case examples described in this book come from the field of business analytics, industry, medical informatics and related fields. I thought it important to select examples that I could document, from reliable sources. Consequently, the reference section is enriched with articles from journals, newspaper articles, and books. Most of these cited articles are available for free Web download.

Chapter 2: FACTS AND FIGURES OF BIG DATA

Surprising Statistics about Big Data

Baseline has reported extensively about the booming interest in big data. In fact, seven out of 10 CIOs and other top executives say data analytics is a "crucial" or "very important" business driver, according to survey research from KPMG. The interest is fueled by the fact that big data continues to grow so rapidly: A statistic quoted in an IDC and

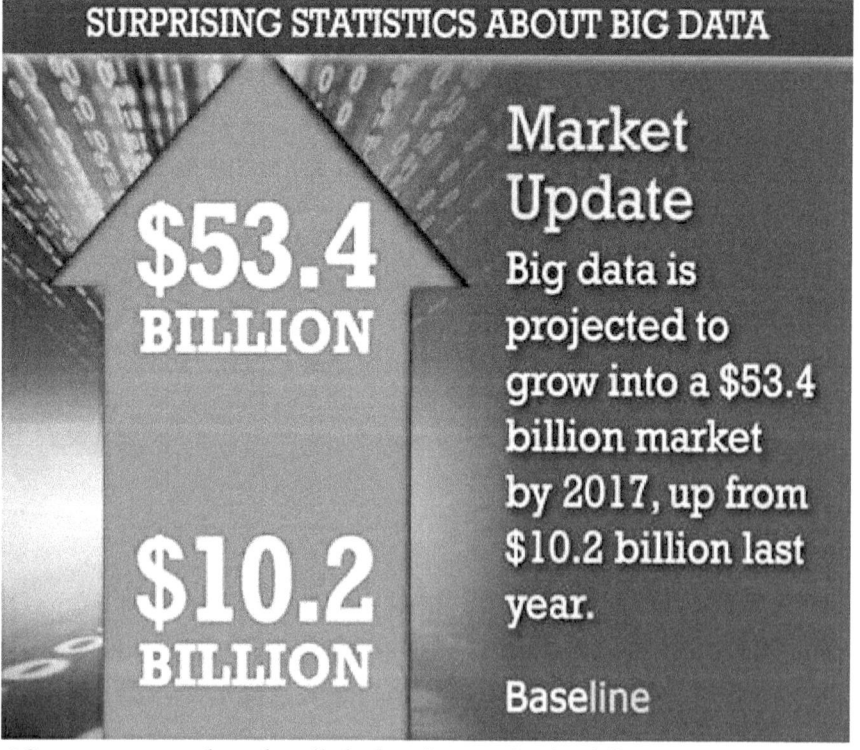

EMC report says that the digital universe is doubling every two years, and will reach 40,000 exabytes (40 trillion gigabytes) by 2020. (A

single exabyte of storage can contain 50,000 years' worth of DVD-quality video.) As a result, a growing number of corporations have access to far more information that they can manage, and they are constantly challenged with getting the right IT tools and tech talent in place to maximize big data's value. As with any new initiatives, however, there will always be pushback. So, if you're trying to justify the need for a big data initiative, consider using the following impressive statistics, which were obtained from research produced or compiled by Sybase, the Wikibon Project, Capgemini, CSC and other organizations.   By Dennis   McCafferty | Posted   2014-02-18 (http://www.baselinemag.com/analytics-big-data/slideshows/ surprising-statistics-about-big-data.html#sthash.K0mcOHk2.dpuf)

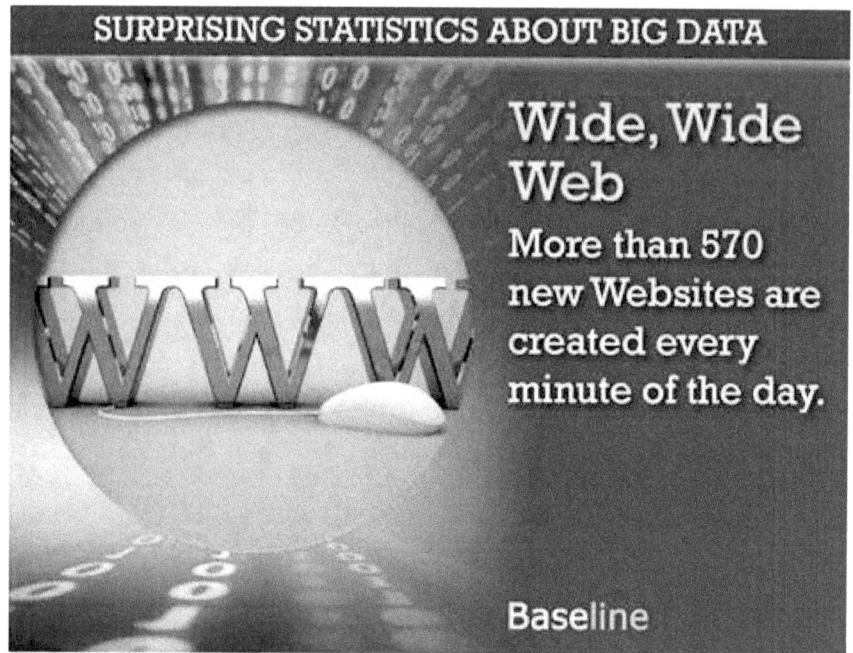

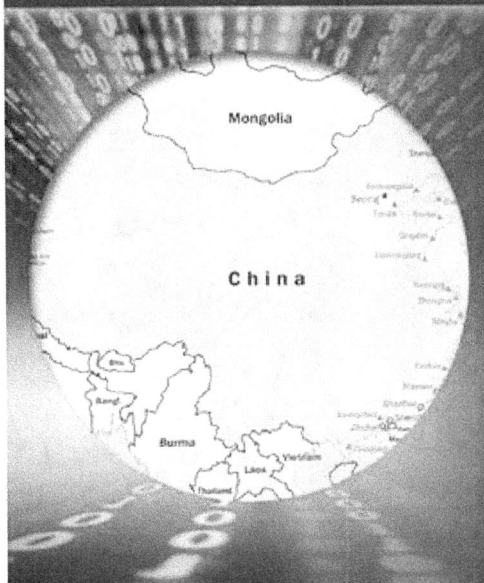

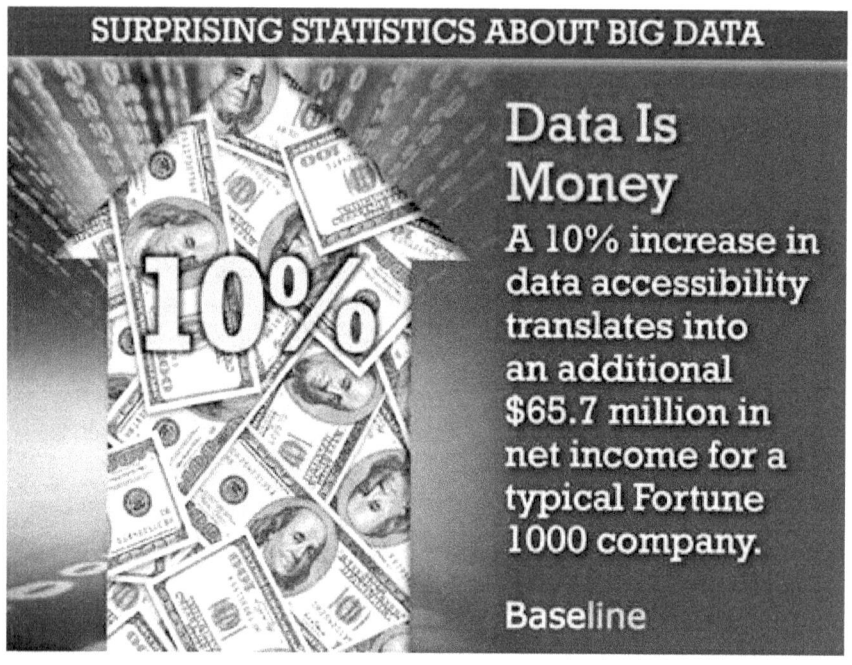

See more at: http://www.baselinemag.com/analytics-big-data/ slideshows/surprising-statistics-about-big-data.html#sthash.QlnaTg6T.dpuf/

http://www.baselinemag.com/analytics-big-data/slideshows/ surprising-statistics-about-big-data.html

Big data is growing

Big data is growing, in fact, the sector is growing so fast and we are producing data so voraciously, that no one can afford to ignore it as a "fad" any more. And, it's going to affect all companies, large and small, across all segments of the market — from healthcare to public safety, and retail to wholesale. Big data is changing the world as we know it. If you don't believe me, check out some of these (frankly staggering) statistics:

- **60%** - One study suggests that retailers who fully leverage the power of big data could see an increase in their operating margins by as much as 60 percent! (Source: http://www. mckinsey.com/insights/business_technology/ getting_big_impact_from_big_data?cid=other-eml-alt-mkq-mck-oth-1501).

- **4.4 million** - That's how many IT jobs there will be internationally in the big data field by the end of 2015, and it's estimated that 1.9 million of these jobs will be in the U.S. alone. It also suggests that there will be a large gap between the number of jobs available and the number of skilled workers to fill those jobs. (Source: http://www.statista.com/statistics/255952/ number-of-big-data-jobs-in-us-and-globally/).

- **$3.4 billion** - The advanced and predictive analytics (APA) software market is expected to grow to $3.4 billion worldwide by 2018. (Source: http://www.idc.com/getdoc.jsp?containerId=249054).

- **$8 million** - In one study, the average business expected to spend $8 million this year on big data and related projects. (Source: https://www.atkearney.com/analytics/featured-article/-/asset_ publisher/FNSUwH9BGQyt/content/beyond-big-the-analytically-powered-organization/10192).

- **$50.1 billion** - Big Data was a $28.5B market in 2014, growing to $50.1 billion overall in 2015. (Source: http://wikibon.org/wiki/v/Big_Data_Vendor_Revenue_ and_Market_Forecast_2013-2017).

- **5 times more likely** - Companies that use big data analytics are five times more likely to make decisions "much faster" than their competition. (Source: http://www.forbes.com/ sites/louiscolumbus/2014/06/24/roundup-of-analytics-big-data-business-intelligence-forecasts-and-market-estimates-2014/).

- **$65.7 million** - As little as a 10 percent increase in the accessibility of data can mean an additional $65.7 million net income for a typical Fortune 1000 company. (Source: http://www. baselinemag.com/analytics-big-data/slideshows/surprising-statistics-about-big-data.html#sthash.EBPgNL3T.dpuf).

- **$200 million** - The Obama administration is investing more than $200 million in big data initiatives. (Source: http://www. baselinemag.com/analytics-big-data/slideshows/surprising-statistics-about-big-data.html).

- **90 percent** - Ninety percent of the data in existence was created in the last two years. (Source: http://www.baselinemag.com/analytics-big-data/slideshows/surprising-statistics-about-big-data.html).

- **$3.57 billion** - Customer experience enhancement is expected to be the largest big data business category, and the one with the most growth, with forecasts saying this sector will grow from $0.75 billion in 2015 to $3.57 billion in 2020.

- **26 hours** - Macy's has reportedly been able to save 26 hours every time it optimizes pricing for its 73 million products through use of big data, allowing them to change pricing more frequently to follow retail trends. (Source: http://www.big-dataforum.com/1174/saving-time-money-big-data).

- **$500 billion** - One study suggests that the U.S. government could save $500 billion *annually* by implementing big data projects. (Source: http://www.meritalk.com/smarterunclesam).

Studies also show that companies (especially small and medium sized companies) put cost and personnel problems as the top reasons they *haven't* implemented big data projects yet, but these projects need to become priority fast, or those companies risk being left behind. (http://www.smartdatacollective.com/bernardmarr/325698/big-data-amazing-numbers-2015).

The Rapid Growth of Unstructured Data

- YouTube users upload 48 hours of new video every minute of the day. (Source: http://wikibon.org/blog/big-data-infographics/)
- 571 new websites are created every minute of the day. (Source: http://wikibon.org/blog/big-data-infographics/)
- Brands and organizations on Face book receive 34,722 Likes every minute of the day. (Source: http://wikibon.org/blog/big-data-infographics/)
- 100 terabytes of data uploaded daily to Face book. (Source: http://wikibon.org/blog/big-data-infographics/)
- According to Twitter's own research in early 2012, it sees roughly 175 million tweets every day, and has more than 465 million accounts. (Source: http://www.mediapost.com/publications/ article/173109/a-conversation-on-the-role-of-big-data-in-marketin.html)
- 30 Billion Pieces of content shared on Face book every month. (Source: http://www.mckinsey.com/insights/business_technology/big_data_the_next_frontier_for_innovation)
- Data production will be 44 times greater in 2020 than it was in 2009. (Source: http://wikibon.org/blog/big-data-infographics/)
- In late 2011, IDC Digital Universe published a report indicating that some 1.8 zettabytes of data will be created

that year. (Source: https://www.siliconrepublic.com/ companies/2003/11/19/ security-giants-team-up-to-defeat-virus-threats)

In other words, the amount of data in the world today is equal to:

o   Every person in the US tweeting three tweets per minute for 26,976 years.

o   Every person in the world having more than 215m high-resolution MRI scans a day.

o   More than 200bn HD movies – this would take a person 47m years to watch.

17 Big Data and Analytics Developments You Overlooked

By JOE PANETTIERI, JUN 5, 2015 10:00am ET (http://www.information-management.com/sdm/2001510.html)

A look at the latest big data, business analytics and business intelligence developments for the week ending June 5, 2015:

1. Attunity Ltd. (http://www.attunity.com/) has pushed into the NoSQL data protection market. The company's latest offering, Attunity Replicate for MongoDB (http://www.attunity.com/news/attunity-expands-big-data-solution-support-fast-growing-nosql-market), automates data loading and replication between databases, data warehouses, Hadoop and MongoDB.

2. Beyondsoft Consulting North America is buying Piraeus Consulting (http://www.beyondsoft.com/node/1637), a management consulting and business intelligence firm, for up to $7.5 million.

3. BlueData (http://www.bluedata.com/) announced support for Docker containers, allowing enterprise IT organizations to deploy Apache Hadoop or Apache Spark in a lightweight container environment. Data scientists and developers can now download BlueData EPIC Lite (http://info.bluedata.com/EPIC_Lite_Download_Request.html) -- a free version of the EPIC platform available immediately -- to spin up virtual Hadoop or Spark clusters in Docker containers on their laptop, the company said.

4. Couch base is connecting the dots between the SQL query language and NoSQL databases (http://www.couchbase.com/press-releases/   couchbase-introduces-n1ql-breakthrough-query-language). The effort strives to make it easier for developers to build web, mobile and IoT apps. Couch base collaborated with the University of California San Diego on this new technology. Informatics and Tableau are building connectors and integrations to Couch base's new query language.

5. DataScience (http://datascience.com/), which offers enterprise data analytics services, rose $4.5 million in a Series A funding. The round was led by Greycroft Partners.

6. Datameer (http://www.datameer.com/company/news/press-releases/   datameer-delivers-comprehensive-governance-for-hadoop-analytics.html) announced new data governance capabilities for its native Hadoop environment. The improvements aim to assist customers with mission-critical and regulatory-compliant analytics use cases, Datameer said.

7. Gild (http://www.gild.com/) launched a business intelligence (BI) solution for hiring, applying predictive analytics and insight to the hiring process.

8. Illinois Business Intelligence (IBI- http://www. illinoisbusinessintelligence.org/), a new service offered through Illinois State University's Stevenson Center for Community and Economic Development, provides free, customized market research intelligence and referrals to small businesses and entrepreneurs, the university said.

9. IneoQuest Technologies (http://www.ineoquest.com/) is integrating its behavioral video analytics with **Anritsu's** eoSight and eoLive suite of products for customer experience analytics. Anritsu provides service assurance and customer analytics solutions for global communication systems and operators.

10. Izenda (http://www.izenda.com/) launched version 6.9 of its business intelligence platform. The offering "makes dashboard design and view customization easy for users with its controls all in one place, enhancing the control and functionality of Izenda's embedded, self-service business intelligence and analytics platform." Izenda's platform delivers ad-hoc reports and dashboards, data visualizations and forms, the company said.

11. The **UK government** unveiled a £313 million partnership with **IBM** to boost big data research in that country. The effort involves IBM's Watson platform and support from at least 24 IBM researchers, IBM and the UK government said.

12. LHP Telematics (http://www.forconstructionpros.com/ company/12000569/lhp-telematics) and Hortonworks (http://hortonworks.com/) partnered to provide predictive analytics and big data services to telematics customers.

13. Marchex (http://www.marchex.com/) expanded its Call Analytics platform and presence beyond North America to include coverage in Europe, Canada, Australia and New Zealand.

14. MicroStrategy 10 Secure Enterprise (http://ir.microstrategy. com/releasedetail.cfm?ReleaseID=916472) is now generally available. The analytics platform combines traditional business intelligence functionality with data discovery, mobile analytics and enterprise security, the company said.

15. NetBase (http://www.netbase.com/) a social media analytics company launched NetBase LIVE Pulse Mashup. Designed for the C-suite, the platform combines social analytics with other critical key performance indicators (KPIs) to help executives make data-driven decisions.

16. Progress (https://www.progress.com/) released two new drivers for its Data Direct enterprise data connectivity suite. The new MongoDB and SparkSQL drivers are part of a larger portfolio that supports roughly 200 data sources.

17. Saama Technologies Inc. (http://www.saama.com/), a big data solutions and services company, raised $35 million in funding from Carrick Capital Partners. Saama will use the money to grow its customer base -- which already includes Actelion, Cisco, CSAA Insurance, Delta Dental, Dignity Health, PayPal, Salesforce.com and Unilever.

http://www.information-management.com/news/Big-Data-Analytics-Weekly-Roundup-10027025-1.html

15 Important Big Data Facts for IT Professionals

Open Source Tools for Big Data: Posted February 04, 2014; *By **Vangie Beal** (http://www.webopedia.com/author/Vangie-Beal)*

Keeping track of big data trends, research and statistics gives IT professionals a solid foundation to plan big data projects. Here are 15 important big data facts that every IT professional should know.

Everyone is talking about big data, from the challenges to yearly spending, job creation and even the tools required for big data projects. Many believe big data will help businesses make better decisions — in fact nearly 8 in 10 executives agree or strongly agree to the statement *"if we could harness all of our data, we would be a much stronger business."*

Keeping track of big data trends, research and statistics gives IT professionals a solid foundation to plan big data projects. Webopedia has compiled this list of important big data facts and statistics that every IT professional should know.

Big Data: How Did We Get Here?

2.5 quintillion bytes of data created daily. ~ IBM

1. How Much Data is there?

Every day, we create 2.5 quintillion bytes of data — so much that 90% of the data in the world today has been created in the last two years alone. This data comes from everywhere: sensors used to gather climate information, posts to social media sites, digital pictures and videos, purchase transaction records, and cell phone GPS signals to name a few. (Source: IBM; IBM Big Data – http://www-01.ibm.com/software/data/bigdata/what-is-big-data.html).

2. Structured Versus Unstructured Data

In classifying big data, Tata Consultancy Services Limited (TCS) looked at how much of companies' data was structured versus unstructured, as well as how much was generated internally versus externally.

- 51% of data is structured
- 27% of data is unstructured
- 21% of data is semi-structured

A much higher than anticipated percentage of data was not structured – either unstructured or semi-structured and a little less than a quarter of the data were external. (Source: Tata Consultancy Services Limited; the Emerging Big Returns on Big Data)

Big Data Jobs

Every big data-related role in the U.S. will create employment for three people outside of IT. – Gartner

3. Big Data Generates Jobs

By 2015, 4.4 million IT jobs globally will be created to support big data, generating 1.9 million IT jobs in the United States. Every big data-related role in the U.S. will create employment for three people outside of IT, so over the next four years a total of 6 million jobs in the U.S. will be generated by the information economy. The challenge? There's not enough talent in the industry. (Source: Gartner; Gartner Symposium/ITxpo - http://www.gartner.com/newsroom/id/2207915)

4. The Big Data Talent Shortage

There will be a shortage of talent necessary for organizations to take advantage of big data. By 2018, the United States alone could face a shortage of 140,000 to 190,000 people with deep analytical skills as well as 1.5 million managers and analysts with the know-how to use the analysis of big data to make effective decisions. (Source: McKinsey

Global Institute; Big data: The next frontier for innovation, competition, and productivity - http://www.mckinsey.com/insights/ business_technology/big_data_the_next_frontier_for_innovation)

5. Rethinking Job Roles and Titles

81% percent of IT leaders and 77% of IT professionals believe there is a significant shortage of workers with the skill required to plan, execute and take advantage of the potential of their organization's data assets. Big data projects might mean rethinking job roles and titles, as well as the non-technical skills needed to make the best use of the data. (Source: TEK Systems)

Big Data Challenges and Dilemmas

57% of IT leaders don't always know who owns the data.
~ TEK Systems

6. Disparate Systems

66% of IT leaders and 53% of IT professionals claim their data is stored in disparate systems – and these organizations must build new platforms to accommodate these increased data management needs. (Source: TEK Systems; Big Data...The next frontier)

7. Getting Business Value from Big Data

The biggest challenges to getting business value from big data are as much cultural as they are technological. When asked to rate a list of 16 challenges, companies placed an organizational challenge at the top of the list: getting business units to share information across organizational silos. A close second was a technological issue: dealing with what has become known as the three V's of big data: data volume, velocity and variety. The third challenge was determining which data to use for different business decisions. (Source: Tata Consultancy Services Limited; The Emerging Big Returns on Big Data)

8. Data Quality

More than half of IT leaders (57%) and IT professionals (52%) report they don't always know who owns the data. If one doesn't know who owns the data, there is no one to hold accountable for its quality. As different sources and varieties of data are fused together for big data projects, ensuring the accuracy and quality of the data will be critical to success. (Source: TEK Systems; Big Data...The next frontier)

9. Create a Stronger Business

Comp TIA found that nearly eight in 10 executives responsible for technical or strategic decisions involving data at their organization agree that harnessing all of their enterprise data would result in a stronger business. The survey also found that 93% of survey participants say data is critically important to their business; the same percent believe it will be important in 2014 as well. One of the strongest arguments for investing in data initiatives stems from the following data point: Nearly 8 in 10 executives agree or strongly agree to the statement "if we could harness all of our data, we would be a much stronger business." (Source: Comp TIA; Big Data Insights and Opportunities - http://www.comptia.org/ resources/big-data-insights-and-opportunities?tracking=research/bigdata.aspx)

10. Better Manage Data

Fewer than 1 in 5 businesses report being exactly where they want to be in managing and using data. Granted, this represents a high bar, but even when including those 'very close' to their target, it still leaves a majority of businesses with significant work to do on the data front. (Source: Comp TIA; Big Data Insights and Opportunities -

http://www.comptia.org/resources/big-data-insights-and-opportunities?
tracking=research/bigdata.aspx)

11. Top 3 Big Data Business Drivers

The top three big data business drivers include:

- Speeding time for operational or analytical workloads (39%)

- Increasing competitive advantage with flexibility of data used in business solutions (34%)

- Business requirements for higher levels of advanced analytics (31%).

(Source: EMA and 9sight Consulting; Big Data: Operationalizing the Buzz - http://www.prnewswire.com/news-releases/pentaho-and-ema-reveal-big-data-priorities-for-2014-229084111.html)

Big Data Spending and Implementations

Big data implementations in production rose from 27% in 2012 to 34% in 2013. – EMA/9sight Consulting

12. Big Data Implementations

Big data implementations in production rose from 27% in 2012 to 34.3% in 2013. In addition, 68% of companies are running two or more big data projects as part of their big data initiatives. For companies with an analytics strategy in place, the top business driver was the need to combine sales information into operational analytics (57%). (Source: EMA and 9sight Consulting; Big Data: Operationalizing the Buzz - http://www.prnewswire.com/news-releases/pentaho-and-ema-reveal-big-data-priorities-for-2014-229084111.html)

13. Big Data Tools

80% of responders said they are already using or planning to use dedicated Big Data tools or architectures in their production environment to cope with the influx of massive amounts of data. 56% of respondents indicated they plan to move existing applications from RDBMS to a NoSQL data store. (Source: Giga Spaces; Big data Survey)

14. Big Data Spending

There's a polarity in spending on Big Data, with a minority of companies spending massive amounts and a larger number spending very little. Some 15% of the surveyed companies with Big Data initiatives spent at least $100 million each on them in 2012, and 7% invested at least $500 million. In contrast, nearly one-quarter (24%) spent less than $2.5 million apiece. (Source: Tata Consultancy Services Limited; The Emerging Big Returns on Big Data)

15. Industries Spending the Most on Big Data

Industries spending the most are telecommunications, travel-related, high tech, and banking; life sciences, retail, and energy/resources companies spend the least. (Source: Tata Consultancy Services Limited; The Emerging Big Returns on Big Data)

Based in Nova Scotia, Canada, Vangie Beal has been covering small business, electronic commerce and Internet technology for more than a decade. You can tweet with her online @AuroraGG.

http://www.webopedia.com/quick_ref/important-big-data-facts-for-it-professionals.html

A Comprehensive List of Big Data Statistics

Posted by <u>Wikibon</u> in <u>Analytics</u> (<u>http://wikibon.org/blog/ category/analytics/</u>), <u>Big Data</u> (<u>http://wikibon.org/blog/category/big-data/</u>) on August 1, 2012.

The team at Wikibon is pretty excited about the future of Big Data. From <u>Big Data infographics</u> (<u>http://wikibon.org/blog/ category/big-data/</u>) to <u>revenue forecasts</u> (<u>http://wikibon.org/wiki/v/ Big_Data_Market_Size_and_ Vendor_Revenues</u>) and <u>funding reports</u> (<u>http://wikibon.org/wiki/v/Big_Data_Start-up_Funding_by_Vendor</u>), to our own <u>Big Data Manifesto</u> (<u>http://wikibon.org/wiki/v/ Big_Data:_Hadoop,_Business_Analytics_and_Beyond</u>), the market is literally exploding with innovation and development. But the sheer magnitudes of the numbers we're analyzing around Big Data are tremendous in and of themselves.

Here are **over thirty significant Big Data statistics** to consider, broken out by the current environment, the growth of unstructured (user generated) data, the marketplace, and business issues related to Big Data.

Innovation Enterprise has compiled a top 30 list for individuals in big data that have had a large impact on the development or popularity of the industry.

Here is an interesting list of top 30 people (actually 34) in Big Data & Analytics, created by Innovation Enterprise.

Unlike other lists, this is not based on Twitter or social media, but also on contributing directly to the industry, and focuses on those who had important parts to play in its growth and sustained popularity.

1. Doug Cutting (https://en.wikipedia.org/wiki/Doug_Cutting) and Mike Cafarella (https://en.wikipedia.org/wiki/Mike_Cafarella), for creating Hadoop

2. Sergey Brin (https://en.wikipedia.org/wiki/Sergey_Brin) and Larry Page (https://en.wikipedia.org/wiki/Larry_Page), founders of Google

3. Edward Snowden, NSA Whistleblower

4. Rob Bearden (http://hortonworks.com/about-us/management-team/), founder of Horton works

5. Kirk D. Borne (https://www.linkedin.com/in/kirkdborne), professor and co-creator of the field of astro informatics

6. Stephen Wolfram (https://en.wikipedia.org/wiki/Stephen_Wolfram), creator of Mathematica and Wolfram Alpha

7. Rich Miner (https://www.gv.com/team/rich-miner) co-founders of Android and a pioneer in the mobile space.

8. Jamie Miller (http://www.ge.com/about-us/leadership/profiles/jamie-s-miller), CIO at GE

9. DJ Patil (https://www.linkedin.com/in/dpatil), a data science pioneer, coined the term "data scientist" with Jeff Hammer bacher

10. Monica Rogati (https://www.linkedin.com/in/mrogati), VP of Data at Jawbone

11. <u>Jeff Smith</u> (https://www.linkedin.com/pub/jeff-smith/a/ 3a4/ 901?trk=pub-pbmap), CIO at IBM

12. <u>Jeff Bezos</u> (https://en.wikipedia.org/wiki/Jeff_Bezos), founder and CEO of Amazon

13. <u>Andy Palmer</u> (https://www.linkedin.com/in/andypalmer), co-founder and CEO of TamR

14. <u>Gregory Piatetsky-Shapiro</u> (https://en.wikipedia.org/wiki/ Gregory_I._Piatetsky-Shapiro), co-founder of KDD and SIGKDD, KDnuggets President

15. <u>Sverre Jarp</u> (http://openlab.web.cern.ch/about/people/ sverre-jarp), ex-CTO at CERN open lab

16. <u>Tom Reilly</u> (https://www.linkedin.com/in/tjreilly), CEO at Cloudera

17. <u>Tom Davenport</u> (https://en.wikipedia.org/wiki/Thomas_ H._Davenport), thought leader and author in analytics and business process innovation

18. <u>John Schroeder</u> (https://www.mapr.com/blog/author/john-schroeder), and <u>M. C. Srivas</u> (https://www.linkedin.com/ pub/m-c-srivas/1/b27/ 41b), co-founders of MapR

19. <u>Scott Howe</u> (https://www.linkedin.com/pub/scott-howe/ 20/864/8a), President and CEO at Acxiom

20. <u>Hilary Mason</u> (https://www.linkedin.com/in/hilarymason), was the Chief Scientist at Bitly, founder at Fast Forward Labs

21. <u>Edwina Dunn and Clive Humby</u> (http://www. humbyanddunn.com/), founders of Dunn-humby

22. Anmol   Modan   (https://www.linkedin.com/in/anmolmadan), co-founder and CEO at Ginger.io

23. Chris Towers (https://www.linkedin.com/in/towerschris), head of big data channel at Innovation Enterprise

24. Billy Beane (https://en.wikipedia.org/wiki/Billy_Beane), baseball coach that inspired Moneyball

25. Tim   O'Reilly   (https://en.wikipedia.org/wiki/Tim_O%27Reilly), owner of O'Reilly Media

26. Vadim   Kutsyy   (https://www.linkedin.com/in/kutsyy), head of Inc Data Lab at eBay

27. Warren   Buffett   (https://www.linkedin.com/in/kutsyy), renowned investor

28. Arijit Sengupta (https://www.linkedin.com/in/asengupta), CEO at BeyondCore

29. Gil   Press   (https://www.linkedin.com/in/gilpress),   data science writer at Forbes

30. Paco Nathan (http://liber118.com/pxn/), well-known data blogger

http://www.kdnuggets.com/2015/02/top-30-people-big-data-analytics.html

Big Data in Today's Business and Technology Environment

- 2.7 Zetabytes of data exist in the digital universe today. (Source: https://www.marketingtechblog.com/ibm-big-data-marketing/)

- 235 Terabytes of data has been collected by the U.S. Library of Congress in April 2011. (Source: https://www.marketingtechblog.com/ibm-big-data-marketing/)
- The Obama administration is investing $200 million in big data research projects. (Source: http://wikibon.org/blog/taming-big-data/)
- IDC Estimates that by 2020, business transactions on the internet- business-to-business and business-to-consumer – will reach 450 billion per day. (Source: http://wikibon.org/blog/unstructured-data/)
- Face book stores, accesses, and analyzes 30+ Petabytes of user generated data. (Source: http://wikibon.org/blog/taming-big-data/)
- Akamai analyzes 75 million events per day to better target advertisements. (Source: http://wikibon.org/blog/taming-big-data/)
- 94% of Hadoop users perform analytics on large volumes of data not possible before; 88% analyze data in greater detail; while 82% can now retain more of their data. (Source: http://www.sys-con.com/node/1920943)
- Walmart handles more than 1 million customer transactions every hour, which is imported into databases estimated to contain more than 2.5 petabytes of data. (Source)
- More than 5 billion people are calling, texting, tweeting and browsing on mobile phones worldwide. (Source)
- Decoding the human genome originally took 10 years to process; now it can be achieved in one week. (Source: http://www.economist.com/node/15557443)
- In 2008, Google was processing 20,000 terabytes of data (20 petabytes) a day. (Source: http://techcrunch.com/2008/01/09/google-processing-20000-terabytes-a-day-and-growing/)

- The largest AT&T database boasts titles including the largest volume of data in one unique database (312 terabytes) and the second largest number of rows in a unique database (1.9 trillion), which comprises AT&T's extensive calling records. (Source: http://www. searcheduncovered.com/?dn=searchfusion.com&pid= 9POK8YGH5)

The Market and the Marketers' Challenge with Big Data

- Big data is a top business priority and drives enormous opportunity for business improvement. Wikibon's own study projects that big data will be a $50 billion business by 2017. (Source: http://siliconangle.com/blog/2012/07/13/ studies-confirm-big-data-as-key-business-priority-growth-driver/)
- As recently as 2009 there were only a handful of big data projects and total industry revenues were under $100 million. By the end of 2012 more than 90 percent of the Fortune 500 will likely have at least some big data initiatives under way. (Source)
- Market research firm IDC has released a new forecast that shows the big data market is expected to grow from $3.2 billion in 2010 to $16.9 billion in 2015. (Source: http://statspotting.com/big-data-statistics-16-9-billion-market-by-2015/)
- In the developed economies of Europe, government administrators could save more than €100 billion ($149 billion) in operational efficiency improvements alone by using big data, not including using big data to reduce fraud

and errors and boost the collection of tax revenues. (Source: http://www.mckinsey.com/insights/business_technology/big_data_the_next_frontier_for_innovation)

- Poor data across businesses and the government costs the U.S. economy $3.1 trillion dollars a year. (Source: http://www-new.insightsquared.com/2012/01/7-facts-about-data-quality-infographic/)

- 140,000 to 190,000. Too few people with deep analytical skills to fill the demand of Big Data jobs in the U.S. by 2018. (Source: http://www.mckinsey.com/insights/business_technology/big_data_the_next_frontier_for_innovation)

- 14.9 percent of marketers polled in Crain's B to B Magazine are still wondering "What is Big Data?" (Source: http://www.mckinsey.com/insights/business_technology/big_data_the_next_frontier_for_innovation)

- 39 percent of marketers say that their data is collected "too infrequently or not real-time enough." (Source: http://www.prnewswire.com/news-releases/study-finds-marketers-struggle-with-the-big-data-and-digital-tools-of-today-142312475.html)

- 29 percent report that their marketing departments have "too little or no customer/consumer data." When data is collected by marketers, it is often not appropriate to real-time decision making. (Source: http://www.prnewswire.com/news-releases/ study-finds-marketers-struggle-with-the-big-data-and-digital-tools-of-today-142312475.html)

Big Data & Real Business Issues

- According to estimates, the volume of business data worldwide, across all companies, doubles every 1.2 years. (Source)

- Poor data can cost businesses 20%–35% of their operating revenue. (Source: http://www.fathomdelivers.com/blog/analytics-and-big-data/big-data-facts-and-statistics-that-will-shock-you/)
- Bad data or poor data quality costs US businesses $600 billion annually. (Source: http://www.fathomdelivers.com/blog/analytics-and-big-data/big-data-facts-and-statistics-that-will-shock-you/)
- According to execs, the influx of data is putting a strain on IT infrastructure. 55 percent of respondents reporting a slowdown of IT systems and 47 percent citing data security problems, according to a global survey from Avanade. (Source)
- In that same survey, by a small but noticeable margin, executives at small companies (fewer than 1,000 employees) are nearly 10 percent more likely to view data as a strategic differentiator than their counter parts at large enterprises. (Source)
- Three-quarters of decision-makers (76 per cent) surveyed anticipate significant impacts in the domain of storage systems as a result of the "Big Data" phenomenon. (Source: http://www.btplc.com/news/articles/showarticle.cfm?articleid={74889611-be1c-4f91-bbed-ab9e72e25918})
- A quarter of decision-makers surveyed predict that data volumes in their companies will rise by more than 60 per cent by the end of 2014, with the average of all respondents anticipating a growth of no less than 42 per cent. (Source)
- 40% projected growth in global data generated per year vs. 5% growth in global IT spending. (Source: http://www.mckinsey.com/insights/business_technology/big_data_the_next_frontier_for_innovation)

(Source: http://wikibon.org/blog/big-data-statistics/)

Big data = big bucks

Big data jobs pay quite well. According to Salaries of Data
Scientists   (http://www.informationweek.com/strategic-cio/executive-
insights-and-innovation/big-data-salaries-top-bi-data-warehousing/a/d-
id/1252874), an April 2014 study from Burtch Works, the 2014 mean

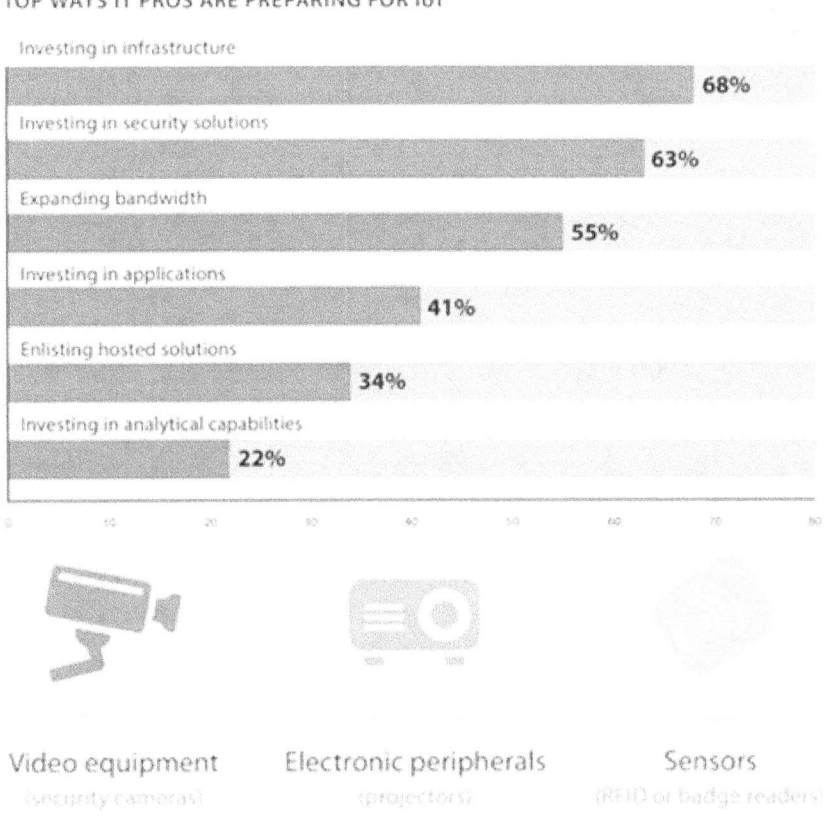

TOP WAYS IT PROS ARE PREPARING FOR IoT

Investing in infrastructure — 68%
Investing in security solutions — 63%
Expanding bandwidth — 55%
Investing in applications — 41%
Enlisting hosted solutions — 34%
Investing in analytical capabilities — 22%

Video equipment (security cameras)   Electronic peripherals (projectors)   Sensors (RFID or badge readers)

base salary for a staff data scientist is $120,000 and $160,000 for a
manager. The estimates are based on interviews with more than 170
data scientists from a Burtch Works employment database. The pay
scale is almost as good for the broader category of big data
professionals, meaning those who "apply sophisticated quantitative

skills to data-describing transactions, interactions, or other behaviors of people to derive insights and prescribe actions." In this category the 2013 median base salary for staff is $90,000; for managers, it's a cool $145,000 (Source: Burtch Works)

10 Powerful Facts about Big Data

Big data means many things to many people, but how broad is its impact? Consider these figures on big data and the gurus who splice it.

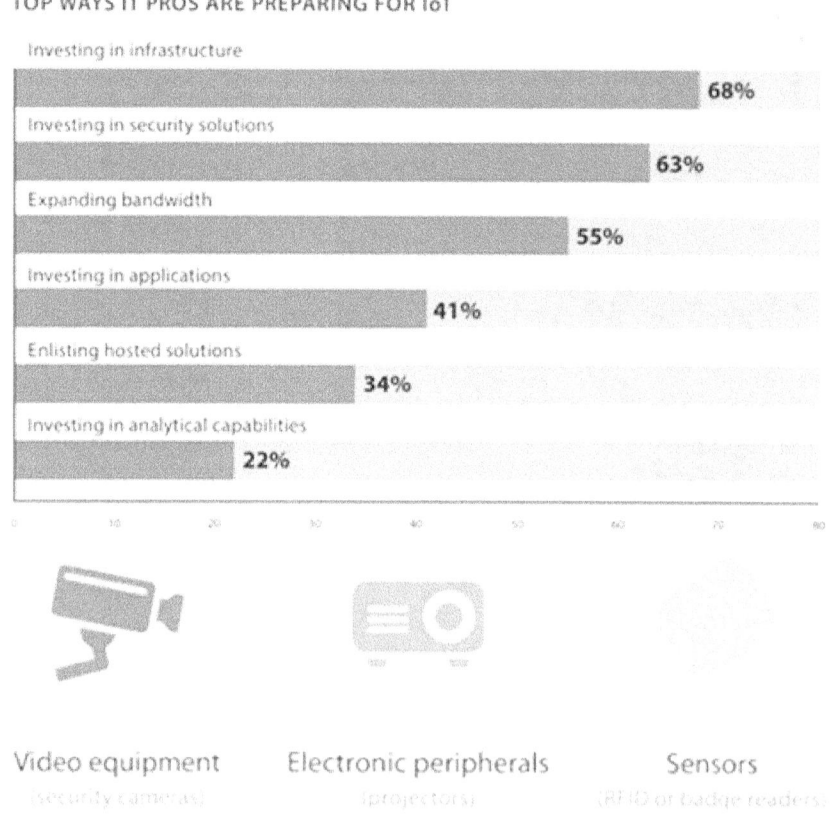

TOP WAYS IT PROS ARE PREPARING FOR IoT

Investing in infrastructure — 68%
Investing in security solutions — 63%
Expanding bandwidth — 55%
Investing in applications — 41%
Enlisting hosted solutions — 34%
Investing in analytical capabilities — 22%

Video equipment (security cameras)   Electronic peripherals (projectors)   Sensors (RFID or badge readers)

Data scientists: still sexy

The eye-grabbing headline of an October 2012 article in the Harvard Business Review called the data science profession the "Sexiest Job of the 21st Century" (https://hbr.org/2012/10/data-scientist-the-sexiest-job-of-the-21st-century/) That's debatable, but if "sexy" is synonymous with "in demand," data scientists haven't lost any of their mojo. According to Modis, a global IT staffing services provider, data scientists remain in "high demand but short supply," which translates into generous six-figure salaries (https://www.pehub.com/2013/02/as-companies-produce-more-data-search-data-scientists-grows-frantic/) for some PhDs with relevant big data experience (Source: Inside Big data - http://insidebigdata.com/2013/04/15/data-scientists-the-new-sex-symbol/)

Be afraid, data warehouse: Hadoop's in town

Should the data warehouse industry fear the rise of Hadoop? Embrace it? That question was posed to two Hadoop pioneers -- Doug Cutting of Cloud era and Arun Murthy of Horton works -- during a Q&A at Hadoop Summit 2014. While many enterprises are moving workloads from data warehouses to Hadoop, that's not happening en masse. But will it? "If you've got a lot of people no longer increasing the size of their data warehouse, but rather capping the size or potentially even decreasing their investment because they find they can do much of the processing as effectively and much more affordably in a Hadoop-based system, I think that's a threat," said Cutting.

(Source: Hadoop Summit)

Privacy fears won't stop big data

The cacophony of concerns rising from a seemingly endless series of privacy and security breaches isn't likely to thwart big data's advancement. The Economist reports in its June 2014 issue that "there is scant evidence that concern about privacy is causing a fundamental change in the way data are used and stored." Gartner analyst Carsten Casper tells the magazine that no "big privacy revolution" is brewing in the IT world. And while companies are asking more privacy-related questions, nine of 10 of those queries have to do with the location of data centers, Casper adds (Source: The Economist).

Big data drives software growth

The compound annual growth rate (CAGR) for the 2013-2018 worldwide software market will hover near 6%, research firm IDC predicts. But big data related categories, including collaborative applications and data access, analysis and delivery solutions, and structured data management software, will show a higher CAGR (around 9%) over that five-year period, says IDC.

A heightened interest in social media will help drive this growth. "This is complementary to the increased attention to big data and analytics solutions, which help enterprises understand and act on anticipated customer behavior and new insights into product reliability and maintenance," said IDC analyst Henry Morris in a statement (Source: IDC - http://www.idc.com/getdoc.jsp?containerId=prUS24907614).

Are big data pros ready for the Internet of Things (IOT)?

Most IT pros say they haven't started preparing for the Internet of Things -- even if they have. Spice works (http://www.spiceworks.com/) polled 440 IT professionals in April 2014 to get their take on the IOT and how they're preparing for it. Sixty-two percent of respondents were in North America and 38% in EMEA (Europe, the Middle East, and Africa). More than half (59%) of respondents said they're not taking specific steps to address the expected data deluge from sensors, cameras, and numerous other IoT devices. However, the survey also found that many IT pros are, in fact, preparing for the IoT by investing in infrastructure, security, applications, analytics, and by expanding bandwidth (Source: Spice works)

Almost everything will be connected

The ***Internet of Things*** will include many strange and wondrous devices, many of which are new to the world of big data. That's why analysts at ABI Research predict more than 30 billion devices (https://www.abiresearch.com/press/more-than-30-billion-devices-will-wirelessly-conne/) will be wirelessly connected by 2020. Health-related data collection will play a large role in the IoT, of course.

Here's a unique example: Microsoft, in conjunction with researchers from the University of Rochester (New York) and University of Southampton (UK), have designed a bra with sensors that detects the wearer's stress level by monitoring heart and skin activity, the BBC reported (http://www.bbc.com/news/technology-25197917). Designed to see if wearable tech can help control stress-related overeating, the bra collects and sends data to a smart phone app to help the user control eating habits (Source: University of Rochester)

20 Shocking Facts and Figures about "Big Data"

By Phil   O   Doherty (https://www.espatial.com/articles/author/philod) October 23, 2012

Here   at eSpatial (https://www.espatial.com/)   we   are   very interested in the subjects surrounding big data, data management and data visualization. After all, our goal is to help businesses and organizations make the most of data of any kind by turning it into engaging and useful visuals. (You can see examples of how we do these here https://www.espatial.com/features/public-maps).

The volume, velocity and variety of data created in the modern digital world are truly astounding.

Here are some facts and figures I've come across in the last while that illustrate that point.

1. The volume of data created by U.S. companies alone each year is enough to fill ten thousand Libraries of Congress. (http://www.sapvirtualevents.com\sapphirenow\sessiondetails.aspx?sId=2310)

2. According to McKinsey – a retailer using big data to the full could increase its operating margin by more than 0%. (http://www.mckinsey.com/Insights/MGI/Research/Technology_and_Innovation/Big_data_The_next_frontier_for_innovation)

3. Zuckerberg noted that 1 billion pieces of content are shared via Face book's Open Graph daily. (http://thenextweb.com/facebook/2012/07/ 26/facebook-says-that-1-billion-pieces-of-content-is-shared-via-open-graph-daily/)

4. Google's Eric Schmidt claims that every two days now we create as much information as we did from the dawn of civilization up until 2003 (http://techcrunch.com/2010/08/04/schmidt-data/)

5. Bad data or poor data quality costs US businesses $600 billion annually. (http://www.fathomdelivers.com/big-data-facts-and-statistics-that-will-shock-you/)

6. According to Gartner Big data will drive $232 billion in spending through 2016. (http://onvab.com/blog/big-data-facts-statistics-trends/)

7. 48 hours of video are uploaded to YouTube every minute, resulting in nearly 8 years of content every day (Source: http://www.pc-wholesale.com/graphics.html)

8. Data collection volume increased by 400% in 2012, from an average of 10 collection events per page to 50 (http://www.krux.com/pro/broadcasts\krux_research\CIS2012/)

9. By 2015, 4.4 million IT jobs globally will be created to support big data, generating 1.9 million IT jobs in the United States (http://www.dailyfinance.com/2012/10/22/gartner-says-big-data-creates-big-jobs-44-million-/)

10. 70% of data is created by individuals – but enterprises are responsible for storing and managing 80% of it. (http://www.csc.com/insights/flxwd/78931-big_data_growth_just_beginning_to_explode).

11. By 2020 one third of all data will be stored, or will have passed through the cloud, and we will have created 35 zetabytes worth of   data (http://www.csc.com/insights/flxwd/78931-big_data_growth_just_beginning_to_ explode)

12. 1.5 million more data-savvy managers are needed to take full   advantage   of   big   data   in   the   United   States (http://www.mckinsey.com/Insights/MGI/Research/Technology_and_Innovation\Big_data_The_next_frontier_for_innovation)

13. There was an estimated 1.8 zettabytes of business data in use   in   2011   up   by   30   percent   from   2010 (http://www.kpmg.com/Global/en/IssuesAndInsights/ArticlesPublications/accelerating-innovation/Documents/ehealth-implementation.pdf)

14. The Obama administration in the US announced $200 million in new R&D investments for "Big Data" initiative in 2012 (http://www.   whitehouse.gov/sites/default/files/microsites\ostp\big_data_press_release.pdf)

15. Big Data is set to create 1.9M IT Jobs in U.S. By 2015 (http://www.cio.com/article/719484/Big_Data_to_Create_1.9M_IT_Jobs_in_U.S._By_2015?taxonomyId=3006)

16. Stacking a pile of CD-ROMs on top of one another until you'd reached the current global storage capacity for digital information would stretch 80,000 km beyond the moon (http://smartdatacollective.com/yellowfin/35139/digital-data-explosion-highlights-need-new-age-database-and-business-intelligence-te)

17. Up to 80% of the 247 billion email messages sent each day is spam (http://www.kurtosys.com/blog/12-big-facts-about-big-data/)

18. There are nearly as many pieces of digital information as there are stars in the universe (Source: http://realcomm.com/advisory/advisoryPrint.asp?AdvisoryID=544)

19. A survey reported that more than 37.5% of large organizations said that analyzing big data is their biggest challenge. (http://www. informationweek.com/big-data/news/big-data-analytics/240005662/big-data-development-challenges-talent-cost-time)

20. Visualization is in demand because it makes data-analysis easier. An InformationWeek Business survey found 45% of the 414 respondents cited "ease-of-use challenges with complex software/less-technically savvy employees" as the second-biggest barrier to adopting BI/analytics products. (http://www.informationweek.com/big-data/commentary/software/business-intelligence/240004277/how-to-choose-advanced-data-visualization-tools)

Data Storage: 21 Interesting Facts & Figures

Posted   by Becca   Burns (http://realcomm.com/advisory/advisoryPrint.asp?AdvisoryID=544) on Wed, Mar, 27, 2013 @ 12:03 PM

The way data is stored is something that every business should be concerned with for it is critical to the security of a business. Would you leave your important documents lying around in an insecure environment? Below are many facts and figures about data storage that a business  owner should know in order to make better informed decisions when it comes to their data.

1. 47% of enterprises cite data growth as one of their top three challenges.

2. According to a recent survey by Forrester Research:

   - 40 percent of enterprises said they plan to spend more on storage hardware in the coming year
   - Another 46 percent saying their spending on storage will be level

☐ Forrester also estimates that storage capacity requirements are growing at a rate of between 15 percent and 25 percent per year.

☐ IT departments will have to manage 50 times the amount of information, 75 times the number of files and 10 times the number of virtual and physical servers, with only 1.5 times the number of IT professionals to manage it all, by 2020. - *Extracting Value from Chaos*

☐ The amount of data stored digitally vs. analog has grown from 1% in 1986 to 94% in 2007.

☐ Gartner report predcts, Big Data in 2013 will drive $34 billion of IT spending, and by 2015, 4.4 million IT jobs will be created to support Big Data.

☐ An Exabyte is 1 billion gigabytes.

☐ Businesses digitally store around 6 Exabyte'sand consumers store about 7 Exabyte's.

☐ One petabyte is about 1 million gigabytes.

☐ Industries and the amount of data they each store:

- Education - 269 petabytes
- Retail - 364 petabytes
- Health Care - 434 petabytes
- Banking - 619 petabytes
- Communications/Media - 715 petabytes
- Government - 848 petabytes
- Manufacturing - 966 petabytes

☐ A few ways stored data is used:

- Retail uses databases to track information for marketing and sales campaigns
- Health Care has databases full of information in order to keep track of important history for each patient
- Manufacturing uses data to evaluate and work machinery to make the production as efficient as possible

☐ The United States ranks the highest for amount of data stored with 3500 petabytes.

☐ Europe is second highest for amount of data stored with 2000 petabytes.

☐ There are four types of storage

- DAS
- NAS
- SAN
- Cloud

☐ DAS (Direct Attached Storage) – computer storage that is directly attached to one computer or server and is not, without special support, directly accessible to other ones.

☐ NAS (Network Attached Storage) - a specialized file server designed specifically to provide centralized data access and storage to heterogeneous network clients.

☐ NAS Benefits:

- Units plug right into existing network switches or hubs
- Runs traditional LAN protocols (typically TCP/IP over Ethernet)
- Supports common file-sharing protocols like NFS for Unix and SMB and CIFS for Windows

☐ SAN (Storage Area Networks) - a set of interconnected drives and servers that acts as a centralized pool of disk storage.

☐ SAN Benefits:

- Simplified management
- Highest possible levels of availability
- Good capacity utilization

☐ Cloud – a use of computing resources (hardware and software) that are delivered as a service over a network (typically the Internet).

☐ Cloud Benefits:

- Allows companies to avoid upfront infrastructure costs, and focus on projects that differentiate their businesses instead of infrastructure
- Allows enterprises to get their applications up and running faster, with improved manageability and less maintenance

- Enables IT to more rapidly adjust resources to meet fluctuating and unpredictable business demand

(http://www.sagiss.com/blog/bid/235984/Data-Storage-21-Interesting-Facts-Figures)

Best Practices for Managing Big Data

Eric Savitz (http://www.forbes.com/fdc/welcome_mjx.shtml), Forbes Staff

Ash Ashutosh (http://www.actifio.com/company/leadership/) is CEO of Actifio (http://www.actifio.com/) *a provider of data management software.*

Big Data is the result of practically everything in the world being monitored and measured; creating data faster than the available technologies can store, process or manage it. Since it is a lot more intuitive to represent information as a "file" than a relational object, there has been a surge of unstructured data, making up as much as 80% of new data we must manage.

Organizations are struggling to manage Big Data. According to IDC, the amount of information created, captured or replicated has exceeded available storage for the first time since 2007. The size of the digital universe this year will be tenfold what it was just five years earlier.

Therefore, organizations must find smarter data management approaches that enable them to effectively corral and optimize their data.

Too many organizations think they can manage Big Data by throwing increasing amounts of storage at the problem. They often buy additional storage capacity every 6-to-12 months, which not only results in exorbitant costs but forces their frazzled IT teams to spend more time on data management rather than more strategic IT initiatives. The lack of a real solution for managing Big Data simply causes tremendous inefficiencies all across the organization.

At the same time, Big Data just keeps growing and growing, according to <u>Forrester   Research</u>   (<u>http://www.forbes.com/fdc/welcome_mjx.shtml</u>):

   – The average organization will grow their data by 50 percent in the coming year.
   – Overall corporate data will grow by a staggering 94 percent.
   – Database systems will grow by 97 percent.
   – Server backups for disaster recovery and continuity will expand by 89 percent.

Big Data results in three basic challenges: storing, processing and managing it efficiently. Scale-out architectures have been developed to store large amounts of data and purpose-built appliances have improved the processing capability. The next frontier is learning how to manage Big Data throughout its entire lifecycle.

What most people don't know is that the vast majority of Big Data is either duplicated data or synthesized data. Let's take a look at a leading medical research facility that generates 100 terabytes of data from various instruments.

This data is then copied by 18 different research departments that further process the data and add 5 terabytes of additional synthesized data each. Now they must manage a total of over a petabyte of data, of which less than 150 terabytes is unique. Yet, the entire petabyte of data is backed up, moved to a disaster recovery site, consuming additional power and space used to store it all. So now, the medical center has used over 10 petabytes of storage to manage less than 150 terabytes of real unique data. This is not efficient.

So how should it be managed?

The first step is to bring the data down to its unique set and reduce the amount of data to be managed.

Next (http://www.forbes.com/companies/next), leverage the power of virtualization technology. Organizations must virtualize this unique data set so that not only multiple applications can reuse the same data footprint, but also the smaller data footprint can be stored on any vendor-independent storage device.

Virtualization is the secret weapon that organizations can wield to battle the Big Data management challenge.

By reducing the data footprint, virtualizing the reuse and storage of the data and centralizing the management of the data set, Big Data is ultimately transformed into small data and managed like virtual data. Now that the data footprint is smaller, organizations will dramatically improve data management in three key areas:

- Less time is required by applications to process data.
- Data can be better secured since the management is centralized, even though access is distributed.
- Results of data analysis are more accurate since all copies of data are visible.

Virtualization is indeed the "hero" when it comes to managing Big Data. And, it gives organizations so many additional benefits – end-users enjoy flexibility, lower costs and freedom from IT vendor lock-in.

A smarter data management approach not only allows Big Data to be backed up far more effectively but also makes it more easily recoverable and accessible with a whopping 90% cost savings - while freeing IT staff to drive more strategic technology initiatives that drive corporate growth instead of engaging in a futile battle with an out-of-control Big Data beast.

Big Data is the result of practically everything in the world being monitored and measured; creating data faster than the available technologies can store, process or manage it. Since it is a lot more intuitive to represent information as a "file" than a relational object, there has been a surge of unstructured data, making up as much as 80% of new data we must manage.

Organizations are struggling to manage Big Data. According to IDC, the amount of information created, captured or replicated has exceeded available storage for the first time since 2007. The size of the digital universe this year will be tenfold what it was just five years earlier.

Therefore, organizations must find smarter data management approaches that enable them to effectively corral and optimize their data.

Too many organizations think they can manage Big Data by throwing increasing amounts of storage at the problem. They often buy additional storage capacity every 6-to-12 months, which not only results in exorbitant costs but forces their frazzled IT teams to spend more time on data management rather than more strategic IT initiatives. The lack of a real solution for managing Big Data simply causes tremendous inefficiencies all across the organization.

At the same time, Big Data just keeps growing and growing, according to Forrester Research (http://blogs.forbes.com/forrester):

- The average organization will grow their data by 50 percent in the coming year.

- Overall corporate data will grow by a staggering 94 percent.
- Database systems will grow by 97 percent.
- Server backups for disaster recovery and continuity will expand by 89 percent.

Big Data results in three basic challenges: *storing, processing and managing it efficiently*. Scale-out architectures have been developed to store large amounts of data and purpose-built appliances have improved the processing capability. The next frontier is learning how to manage Big Data throughout its entire lifecycle.

What most people don't know is that the vast majority of Big Data is either duplicated data or synthesized data. Let's take a look at a leading medical research facility that generates 100 terabytes of data from various instruments.

This data is then copied by 18 different research departments that further process the data and add 5 terabytes of additional synthesized data each. Now they must manage a total of over a petabyte of data, of which less than 150 terabytes is unique. Yet, the entire petabyte of data is backed up, moved to a disaster recovery site, consuming additional power and space used to store it all. So now, the medical center has used over 10 petabytes of storage to manage less than 150 terabytes of real unique data. This is not efficient.

So how should it be managed?

The first step is to bring the data down to its unique set and reduce the amount of data to be managed.

Next (http://www.forbes.com/fdc/welcome_mjx.shtml), leverage the power of virtualization technology. Organizations must virtualize this unique data set so that not only multiple applications can reuse the same data footprint, but also the smaller data footprint can be stored on any vendor-independent storage device.

Virtualization is the secret weapon that organizations can wield to battle the Big Data management challenge.

By reducing the data footprint, virtualizing the reuse and storage of the data and centralizing the management of the data set, Big Data is ultimately transformed into small data and managed like virtual data. Now that the data footprint is smaller, organizations will dramatically improve data management in three key areas:

- Less time is required by applications to process data.
- Data can be better secured since the management is centralized, even though access is distributed.
- Results of data analysis are more accurate since all copies of data are visible.

Virtualization is indeed the "hero" when it comes to managing Big Data. And, it gives organizations so many additional benefits – end-users enjoy flexibility, lower costs and freedom from IT vendor lock-in.

A smarter data management approach not only allows Big Data to be backed up far more effectively but also makes it more easily recoverable and accessible with a whopping 90% cost savings - while freeing IT staff to drive more strategic technology initiatives that drive corporate growth instead of engaging in a futile battle with an out-of-control Big Data beast.

12 Big Data Facts for Marketers in 2014

The idea of Big Data is nothing new, but its potential to solve today's problems and spark innovation is unprecedented.

The Library of Alexandria in ancient Egypt was one of the largest and most significant libraries of the early world. From third century BC until the Roman conquest of Egypt in 30 BC, the Royal Library of Alexandria was accepted as the culmination of human knowledge and culture. Most of the books were written on papyrus; scholars say their combined value was incalculable—much like the large, often hard-to-manage sets of data nowadays.

In fact, researchers today say if all of Alexandria's information were stored on CDs, those stacked discs would create five separate piles that would all reach the moon. In other words, Alexandria was the Big Data storage center of the ancient world.

The idea of <u>Big Data</u> (<u>http://www.dmnews.com/dataanalytics/</u> <u>six-big-data-dos-and-donts/article/343950/</u>) — any collection of data sets that are so large and complex that it becomes difficult to process is nothing new. What is new, however, are the constantly evolving tech tools that marketers use to process that data; the exponential rate at which data's created; its open availability to marketers, private and public organizations, and society as a whole; and the continual innovation and discovery that derives from Big Data.

Today you'll find that information is ruled less by the physical constraints of storage and human ability and led more by tech and digital tools. *Here are 12 data facts that provide a snapshot of the evolution of and conversation around Big Data innovation in 2014.*

1. One third of all data will be stored in or will pass through the cloud by 2020. (Chassis Plans)

2. Dirty data, or poor data quality, costs U.S. businesses **$600 billion** annually. (Fathom)

3. Eighty-three percent of companies have started some sort of Big Data program, although many remain in fledging stages—

especially small businesses that have fewer resources to invest. (Experian Data Quality)

4. San Francisco is ranked the **number one** U.S. city in open data innovation, followed by New York and Boston. (U.S. City Open Data Census)

5. On average, companies collect customer and prospect data from **3.4 channels**. The most common channel for interacting with customers is a company's website, followed by the sales team and then the call center. (Experian Data Quality)

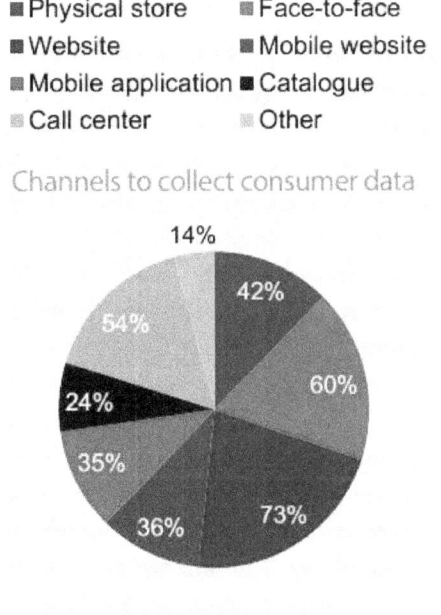

Channels to collect consumer data

6. There are nearly as many pieces of digital information as there are stars in the universe. (Realcomm)

7. Seventy-nine percent of companies have an analytics team. The median number of employees on an analytics team is **22**. (Experian Data Quality)

8. By 2018 the United States alone could face a shortage of 140,000 to **190,000** people with deep analytical skills to fill data-centric jobs. (McKinsey Global Institute)

9. In 2000, just one quarter of the world's stored information was digital. Today, more than **98%** of all stored information is digital. (Foreign Affairs)

10. Brands and organizations receive **34,722** Face book Likes every minute. (Big Data Insight Group)

11. An estimated **80 to 90%** of the data in any organization is unstructured—or doesn't fit neatly in a traditional row-column database. Some examples include email messages, word processing documents, videos, photos, audio files, presentations, and Web pages. (Webopedia)

12. The Big Data market will reach **$16.9 billion** by 2015, up from $3.2 billion in 2010. (International Data Corporation)

(http://www.dmnews.com/12-big-data-facts-for-marketers-in-2014/article/368688/)

Turning Big Data into Major Insight

Kevin Geraghty, SVP of advanced analytics and decision sciences for 360i, explains how marketers can choose which data best fuels their campaigns. Extracting insights from Big Data doesn't have to be complicated. Knowing which data to collect, analyze, and take action on doesn't have to be elusive for marketers. The right data strategy will inevitably solve internal challenges, provide a clearer view of target customers (http://www.dmnews.com/direct-line-blog/how-to-get-a-360-degree-view-of-an-email-subscriber/article/344292/), and fuel effective, engaging campaigns. Kevin Geraghty, SVP of advanced analytics and decision sciences for 360i, explains how marketers can get there. In this revealing Q&A, Geraghty shares how to identify and then zero in on the most relevant data sets to your brand. He also divulges why more marketers should attempt to extract insights in real time.

How can marketers determine what data to collect to inform their campaigns?

The real first step in data collection is bringing together the data scientists with marketers. Then there needs to be a free-flowing, brainstorming approach. Of course, some of the ideas that you think will work, won't at all. There needs to be a sort of testing process and a willingness to fail fast. But you need the right people to do that testing [to find the best way to collect and analyze data] so your team understands what's working or what's just spurious correlation. So, testing and that internal partnership are two important parts of great data collection.

Should marketers take a closer look at open data?

Absolutely, Red Roof Inn is one a number of successful cases (http://www.dmnews.com/red-roof-inn-turns-weather-woes-into-major-sales/ article/359721/) where a brand leveraged open data and the semantic web [the idea that metadata added to Web pages can make them readable for machines]. And there are a couple of key components in the success [of the Red Roof Inn example]. First, there's the real-time aspect of it. This is the one of the challenges marketers have with, for example, government data. It lags behind that market for so long that it can quite often be difficult for businesses to leverage in that sort of real-time marketing space. So one of the things [marketers] need to look for when they're searching through this type of data is whether we can get real-time feeds and [insights] that we can make use of.

The other key thing is [open data's] effectiveness for the business. Here again, we consider collaboration. Any time we're taking on these projects or problems [the team at 360i] sits down our data scientists who know what data is available. Then we tie that together in a conversation with [marketers], or business folks, who really understand what key factors would drive the business. And for a large number of clients, weather is just so important, such as in the case with Red Roof Inn. Marketers can really tailor timing of that marketing [campaign] to the weather.

How important is the speed at which marketers transform information into insight?

I can't envision a world now where you can't be fast. For example, when electricity was first made available, the factories that adopted [the development] quicker gained a competitive advantage. It's the same today—perhaps even more so. Nowadays we're in that transition with real-time data. Right now, it gives [brands] a competitive advantage. If you're not responding to changes, you're just going to get killed…. But what I will say is that speed is not enough in and of itself. If you're responding [to open data] in the wrong way, you're just going to lose money faster. You have to be efficient and fast.

From the September 2014 Issue of Direct Marketing News » (http://www.dmnews.com/issue/september/01/2014/2382/)

http://www.dmnews.com/turning-big-data-into-major-insight/article/364302/

25 Eye-Opening Facts of Big Data Everyone Should Know

We surely see a lot of hype surrounding big data but I believe the following 25 facts speak for themselves and help to paint a realistic picture of the phenomenon we now call 'Big Data' - a phenomenon that is changing the world as we know it.

1. Every 2 days we create as much information as we did from the beginning of time until 2003 [Source http://techcrunch.com/2010/08/04/schmidt-data/]

2. Over 90% of all the data in the world was created in the past 2 years. [Source http://www-01.ibm.com/software/data/bigdata/]

3. It is expected that by 2020 the amount of digital information in existence will have grown from 3.2 zettabytes today to 40 zettabytes. [Source http://barnraisersllc.com/2012/12/38-big-facts-big-data-companies/]

4. The total amount of data being captured and stored by industry doubles every 1.2 years [Source http://www.waterfordtechnologies.com/blog/file-archiving/big-data-interesting-facts/]

5. Every minute we send 204 million emails, generate 1,8 million Face book likes, send 278 thousand Tweets, and up-load 200 thousand photos to Face book [Source http://blog. qmee.com/wp-content/uploads/2013/07/Qmee-Online-In-60-Seconds2.png]

6. Google alone processes on average over 40 thousand search queries per second, making it over 3.5 billion in a single day. [Source http://www.internetlivestats.com/google-search-statistics/]

7. Around 100 hours of video are uploaded to YouTube every minute and it would take you around 15 years to

watch every video uploaded by users in one day. [Source https://www.youtube.com/yt/press/en-GB/statistics.html]

8. Face book users share 30 billion pieces of content between them every day. [Source http://blog.kurtosys.com/12-big-facts-about-big-data/#.VBszDBY4S-J]

9. If you burned all of the data created in just one day onto DVDs, you could stack them on top of each other and reach the moon – twice. [Source: http://www.computerworld.com/article/2469904/cloud-computing/enough-data-to-fill-a-stack-of-dvds-to-the-moon--and-back-.html]

10. AT&T is thought to hold the world's largest volume of data in one unique database – its phone records database is 312 terabytes in size, and contains almost 2 trillion rows. [Source http://www.baselinemag.com/analytics-big-data/slideshows/surprising-statistics-about-big-data.html]

11. 570 new websites spring into existence every minute of every day. [Source http://dazeinfo.com/2014/05/02/rise-big-data-industry-market-worth-53-4-billion-2017/]

12. 1.9 million IT jobs will be created in the US by 2015 to carry out big data projects. Each of those will be supported by 3 new jobs created outside of IT – meaning a total of 6 million new jobs thanks to big data. [Source http://www.webopedia.com/quick_ref/important-big-data-facts-for-it-professionals. html]

13. Today's data centers occupy an area of land equal in size to almost 6,000 football fields. [Source: http://blog.kurtosys.com/12-big-facts-about-big-data/#.VBszDBY4S-J]

14. Between them, companies monitoring Twitter to measure "sentiment" analyze 12 terabytes of tweets every day. [Source: http://barnraisersllc.com/2012/12/38-big-facts-big-data-companies/]

15. The amount of data transferred over mobile networks increased by 81% to 1.5 exabytes (1.5 billion gigabytes) per month between 2012 and 2014. Video accounts for 53% of that total. [Source: http://www.fool.com/investing/general/2014/03/29/10-fascinating-facts-about-the-mobile-internet.aspx]

16. The NSA is thought to analyze 1.6% of all global internet traffic – around 30 petabytes (30 million gigabytes) every day [Source http://www.cnet.com/uk/news/nsa-claims-it-touches-only-1-6-percent-of-internet-traffic/]

17. The value of the Hadoop market is expected to soar from $2 billion in 2013 to $50 billion by 2020, according to market research firm Allied Market Research. [Source http://www.   datanami.com/2014/05/29/hadoop-market-grow-58-2020-report-says/]

18. The number of Bits of information stored in the digital universe is thought to have exceeded the number of stars in the physical universe in 2007. [Source http://www.computerworld.com/article/2537648/data-center/study--digital-universe-and-its-impact-bigger-than-we-thought.html]

19. This year, there will be over 1.2 billion smart phones in the world (which are stuffed full of sensors and data collection features), and the growth is predicted to continue. [Source http://www.zdnet.com/article/idc-smartphone-growth-to-continue-reach-1-2-billion-in-2014/]

20. The boom of the Internet of Things will mean that the amount of devices that connect to the Internet will rise from about 13 billion today to 50 billion by 2020. [Source http://newsroom.cisco.com/ioe]

21. 12 million RFID tags – used to capture data and track movement of objects in the physical world – had been sold in by 2011. By 2021, it is estimated that number will have risen to 209 billion as the Internet of Things takes off. [Source http://www.chassis-plans.com/blog/big-data-interesting-facts-and-figures/]

22. Big data has been used to predict crimes before they happen – a "predictive policing" trial in California was able to identify areas where crime will occur three times more accurately than existing methods of forecasting. [Source http://www.businessinsider.com/the-lapd-is-predicting-where-crime-will-occur-based-on-computer-analysis-2014-6?IR=T]

23. By better integrating big data analytics into healthcare, the industry could save $300bn a year, according to a recent report – that's the equivalent of reducing the healthcare costs of every man, woman and child by $1,000 a year. [Source http://wikibon.org/blog/big-data-statistics/]

24. Retailers could increase their profit margins by more than 60% through the full exploitation of big data analytics. [Source http://www.mckinsey.com/insights/business_technology/big_data_the_next_frontier_for_innovation]

25. The big data industry is expected to grow from US$10.2 billion in 2013 to about US$54.3 billion by 2017. [Source

http://dazeinfo.com/2014/05/02/rise-big-data-industry-market-worth-53-4-billion-2017/]

I hope you found these facts interesting, inspiring and may be a little scary?

Big Data: Interesting Facts and Figures (Fun facts)

There is a lot of talk in the media about "Big Data." Here are some fun facts on the subject:

It took from the dawn of civilization to the year 2003 for the world to generate 1.8 zettabytes (10 to the 12th gigabytes) of data. In 2011 it took two days on average to generate the same amount of data.

- In the year 2011 there were 12 million RFID tags sold worldwide. That number is projected to be 209 billion by 2021.
- There are 750 million photos uploaded to Facebook every two days
- 1/3 of all data will be stored in or pass through the cloud by the year 2020 and will amount to 35 zettabytes of combined data
- There are almost as may bits of information in the digital universe as there are stars in our real universe.
- There are over 247 billion e-mail messages sent each day. Up to 80% of them are spam.
- 48 hours of video are uploaded to YouTube every minute, resulting in 8 years' worth of digital content each day
- The world's data doubles every two years
- Oil drilling platforms have 20,000 to 40,000 sensors
- The number of text messages sent and received every day exceeds the population of the planet
- Twitter processes 7 terabytes of data every day

94

- Face book processes 10 terabytes of data every day
- Decoding the human genome took 10 years to process; now it can be accomplished in one week
- 571 new websites are created every minute of the day
- U.S. drone aircraft sent back 24 years with of video footage in 2009
- Google has over 3 million servers processing over 1.7 trillion searches per year in 2011 (22 million in 2000)
- Data centers consume up to 1.5 percent of all the electricity in the world

Source: (http://www.chassis-plans.com/blog/big-data-interesting-facts-and-figures/)

November 8, 2012 | Feature Article (http://www.news-sap.com/topics/feature-article/) | by Shandy Lo (http://www.news-sap.com/author/shandylo/)

Chapter 3: FIFTY TOP OPEN SOURCE TOOLS FOR BIG DATA

Whenever analysts or journalists assemble lists of the top trends for this year, "big data" is almost certain to be on the list. While the catchphrase is fairly new, in one sense, big data isn't really a new concept. Computers have always worked with large and growing sets of data, and we've had databases and data warehouses for years.

What is new is how much bigger that data is, how quickly it is growing and how complicated it is. Enterprises understand that the data in their systems represents a gold mine of insights that could help them improve their processes and their performance. But they need tools that will allow them to collect and analyze that data.

Not surprisingly, the big data market is growing very quickly in response to the growing demand from enterprises. According to IDC, the market for big data products and services was worth $3.2 billion in 2010, and they predict the market will grow to hit $16.9 billion by 2015. That's a 39.4 percent annual growth rate, which is seven times higher than the growth rate IDC expects for the IT market as a whole.

Interestingly, many of the best and best known big data tools available are open source projects. The very best known of these is Hadoop, which is spawning an entire industry of related services and products. This month, we're profiling Hadoop, as well as 49 other big data projects. Here you'll find a lot of Apache projects related to Hadoop, as well as open source NoSQL databases, business intelligence tools, development tools and much more.

Big Data Analysis Platforms and Tools

1. Hadoop (http://hadoop.apache.org/)

You simply can't talk about big data without mentioning Hadoop. The Apache distributed data processing software is so pervasive that often the terms "Hadoop" and "big data" are used synonymously. The Apache Foundation also sponsors a number of related projects that extend the capabilities of Hadoop, and many of them are mentioned below. In addition, numerous vendors offer supported versions of Hadoop and related technologies. Operating System: Windows, Linux, OS X.

2. MapReduce

Originally developed by Google, the MapReduce website describe it as "a programming model and software framework for writing applications that rapidly process vast amounts of data in parallel on large clusters of compute nodes." It's used by Hadoop, as well as many other data processing applications. Operating System: OS Independent.

3. GridGain (http://www.gridgain.com/)

GridGrain offers an alternative to Hadoop's MapReduce that is compatible with the Hadoop Distributed File System. It offers in-memory processing for fast analysis of real-time data. You can download the open source version from GitHub or purchase a commercially supported version from the link above. Operating System: Windows, Linux, OS X.

4. HPCC (http://hpccsystems.com/)

Developed by LexisNexis Risk Solutions, HPCC is short for "high performance computing cluster." It claims to offer superior performance to Hadoop. Both free community versions and paid enterprise versions are available. Operating System: Linux.

5. Storm (https://github.com/nathanmarz/storm#readme)

Now owned by Twitter, Storm offers distributed real-time computation capabilities and is often described as the "Hadoop of real time." It's highly scalable, robust, fault-tolerant and works with nearly all programming languages. Operating System: Linux.

Databases/Data Warehouses

6. Cassandra (http://cassandra.apache.org/)

Originally developed by Face book, this NoSQL database is now managed by the Apache Foundation. It's used by many organizations with large, active datasets, including Netflix, Twitter, Urban Airship, Constant Contact, Reddit, Cisco and Digg. Commercial support and services are available through third-party vendors (http://wiki.apache.org/cassandra/ThirdPartySupport).   Operating System: OS Independent.

7. HBase (http://hbase.apache.org/)

Another Apache project, HBase is the non-relational data store for Hadoop. Features include linear and modular scalability, strictly consistent reads and writes automatic failover support and much more. Operating System: OS Independent.

8. MongoDB (https://www.mongodb.org/)

MongoDB was designed to support hu**mongo**us databases. It's a NoSQL database with document-oriented storage, full index support, replication and high availability, and more. Commercial support is available   through 10gen   (https://www.mongodb.com/lp/contact/enterprise). Operating system: Windows, Linux, OS X, Solaris.

9. Neo4j (http://neo4j.com/)

The "world's leading graph database," Neo4j boasts performance improvements up to 1000x or more versus relational databases. Interested organizations can purchase advanced or enterprise versions from Neo Technology. Operating System: Windows, Linux.

10. CouchDB (http://couchdb.apache.org/)

Designed for the Web, CouchDB stores data in JSON documents that you can access via the Web or query using JavaScript. It offers distributed scaling with fault-tolerant storage. Operating system: Windows, Linux, OS X, Android.

11. OrientDB (http://orientdb.com/)

This NoSQL database can store up to 150,000 documents per second and can load graphs in just milliseconds. It combines the flexibility of document databases with the power of graph databases, while supporting features such as ACID transactions, fast indexes, native and SQL queries, and JSON import and export. Operating system: OS Independent.

12. Terrastore (https://code.google.com/p/terrastore/)

Based on Terracotta, Terrastore boasts "advanced scalability and elasticity features without sacrificing consistency." It supports custom data partitioning, event processing, push-down predicates, range queries, map/reduce querying and processing and server-side update functions. Operating System: OS Independent.

13. FlockDB (https://github.com/twitter/flockdb)

Best known as Twitter's database, FlockDB was designed to store social graphs (i.e., who is following whom and who is blocking whom). It offers horizontal scaling and very fast reads and writes. Operating System: OS Independent.

14. Hibari (http://hibari.github.io/hibari-doc/)

Used by many telecom companies, Hibari is a key-value, big data store with strong consistency, high availability and fast performance. Support is available through Gemini Mobile (http://www.geminimobile.com/). Operating System: OS Independent.

15. Riak

Riak humbly claims to be "the most powerful open-source, distributed database you'll ever put into production." Users include Comcast, Yammer, Voxer, Boeing, SEOMoz, Joyent, Kiip.me, DotCloud, Formspring, the Danish Government and many others. Operating System: Linux, OS X.

16. Hypertable (http://hypertable.org/)

This NoSQL database offers efficiency and fast performance that result in cost savings versus similar databases. The code is 100 percent open source, but paid support is available. Operating System: Linux, OS X

17. BigData (http://www.systap.com/bigdata.htm)

This distributed database can run on a single system or scale to hundreds or thousands of machines. Features include dynamic sharding, high performance, high concurrency, high availability and more. Commercial support is available. Operating System: OS Independent.

18. Hive (http://hive.apache.org/)

Hadoop's data warehouse, Hive promises easy data summarization, ad-hoc queries and other analysis of big data. For queries, it uses a SQL-like language known as HiveQL. Operating System: OS Independent.

19. InfoBright Community Edition (http://www.infobright.org/)

This scalable data warehouse supports data stores up to 50TB and offers "market-leading" data compression up to 40:1 for improved performance. Commercial products based on the same technology can be found at InfoBright.com (https://www.infobright.com/). Operating System: Windows, Linux.

20. Infinispan (http://infinispan.org/)

Infinispan from JBoss describes itself as an "extremely scalable, highly available data grid platform." Java-based, it was designed for multi-core architecture and provides distributed cache capabilities. Operating System: OS Independent.

21. Redis (http://redis.io/)

Sponsored by VMware, Redis offers an in-memory key-value store that can be saved to disk for persistence. It supports many of the most popular programming languages. Operating System: Linux.

Business Intelligence

22. Talend (http://www.talend.com/)

Talend makes a number of different business intelligence and data warehouse products, including Talend Open Studio for Big Data, which is a set of data integration tools that support Hadoop, HDFS, Hive, Hbase and Pig. The company also sells an enterprise edition and other commercial products and services. Operating System: Windows, Linux, OS X.

23. Jaspersoft (http://www.jaspersoft.com/)

Jaspersoft boasts that it makes "the most flexible, cost effective and widely deployed business intelligence software in the world." The link above primarily discusses the commercial versions of its applications, but you can find the open source versions, including the Big Data Reporting Tool atJasperForge.org. Operating System: OS Independent.

24. Palo BI Suite/Jedox (http://forum.jedox.com/)

The open source Palo Suite includes an OLAP Server, Palo Web, Palo ETL Server and Palo for Excel. Jedox offers commercial software based on the same tools. Operating System: OS Independent.

25. Pentaho (http://www.pentaho.com/)

Used by more than 10,000 companies, Pentaho offers business and big data analytics tools with data mining, reporting and dashboard capabilities. See the Pentaho Community Wiki (http://wiki.pentaho. com/display/COM/Community+Wiki+Home) for easy access to the open source downloads. Operating System: Windows, Linux, OS X.

26. SpagoBI

SpagoBI claims to be "the only entirely open source business intelligence suite." Commercial support, training and services are available. Operating System: OS Independent.

27. KNIME (http://www.knime.org/)

The Konstanz Information Miner, or KNIME, offers user-friendly data integration, processing, analysis, and exploration. In 2010, Gartner named KNIME a "Cool Vendor" in analytics, business intelligence, and performance management. In addition to the open source desktop version, several commercial versions are also available. Operating System: Windows, Linux, OS X.

28. BIRT/Actuate   (http://www.eclipse.org/birt/)   / (http://www.actuate.com/)

Short for "Business Intelligence and Reporting Tools," BIRT is an Eclipse-based tool that adds reporting features to Java applications. Actuate is a company that co-founded BIRT and offers a variety of software based on the open source technology. Operating System: OS Independent.

Data Mining

29. RapidMiner/RapidAnalytics (https://rapidminer.com/)

RapidMiner claims to be "the world-leading open-source system for data and text mining." RapidAnalytics is a server version of that product. In addition to the open source versions of each, enterprise versions and paid support are also available from the same site. Operating System: OS Independent.

30. Mahout (http://mahout.apache.org/)

This Apache project offers algorithms for clustering, classification and batch-based collaborative filtering that run on top of Hadoop. The project's goal is to build scalable machine learning libraries. Operating System: OS Independent.

31. Orange (http://orange.biolab.si/)

This project hopes to make data mining "fruitful and fun" for both novices and experts. It offers a wide variety of visualizations, plus a toolbox of more than 100 widgets. Operating System: Windows, Linux, OS X.

32. Weka (http://www.cs.waikato.ac.nz/~ml/weka/)

Short for "Waikato Environment for Knowledge Analysis," Weka offers a set of algorithms for data mining that you can apply directly to data or use in another Java application. Its part of a larger machine learning project and it's also sponsored by Pentaho. Operating System: Windows, Linux, OS X.

33. jHepWork (http://jwork.org/jhepwork/)

Also known as "jWork," this Java-based project provides scientists, engineers and students with an interactive environment for scientific computation, data analysis and data visualization. It's frequently used in data mining, as well as for mathematics and statistical analysis. Operating System: OS Independent.

34. KEEL (http://keel.es/)

KEEL stands for "Knowledge Extraction based on Evolutionary Learning," and it aims to help uses assess evolutionary algorithms for data mining problems like regression, classification, clustering and pattern mining. It includes a large collection of existing algorithms that it uses to compare and with new algorithms. Operating System: OS Independent.

35. SPMF (http://www.philippe-fournier-viger.com/spmf/)

Another Java-based data mining framework, SPMF originally focused on sequential pattern mining, but now also includes tools for association rule mining, sequential rule mining and frequent itemset mining. Currently, it includes 46 different algorithms. Operating System: OS Independent.

36. Rattle (http://rattle.togaware.com/)

Rattle, the "R Analytical Tool to Learn Easily," makes it easier for non-programmers to use the R language by providing a graphical interface for data mining. It can create data summaries (both visual and statistical), build models, draw graphs, score datasets and more. Operating System: Windows, Linux, OS X

File Systems

37. Gluster (http://www.gluster.org/)

Sponsored by Red Hat, Gluster offers unified file and object storage for very large datasets. Because it can scale to 72 brontobytes, it can be used to extend the capabilities of Hadoop beyond the limitations of HDFS (see below). Operating System: Linux.

38. Hadoop Distributed File System

Using Toad for Oracle in an Agile Environment

Also known as HDFS, this is the primary storage system for Hadoop. It quickly replicates data onto several nodes in a cluster in order to provide reliable, fast performance. Operating System: Windows, Linux, OS X.

Programming Languages

39. Pig/Pig Latin (http://pig.apache.org/)

Another Apache Big Data project, Pig is a data analysis platform that uses a textual language called Pig Latin and produces sequences of Map-Reduce programs. It helps makes it easier to write, understand and maintain programs which conduct data analysis tasks in parallel. Operating System: OS Independent.

40. R (http://www.r-project.org/)

Developed by Bell Laboratories, R is a programming language and an environment for statistical computing and graphics that is similar to S. The environment includes a set of tools that make it easier to manipulate data, perform calculations and generate charts and graphs. Operating System: Windows, Linux, OS X.

41. ECL (http://hpccsystems.com/download/docs/ecl-language-reference)

ECL ("Enterprise Control Language") is the language for working with HPCC. A complete set of tools, including an IDE and a debugger are included in HPCC, and documentation is available on the HPCC site. Operating System: Linux.

Big Data Search

42. Lucene (http://lucene.apache.org/core/)

The self-proclaimed "de facto standard for search libraries," Lucene offers very fast indexing and searching for very large datasets.

In fact, it can index over 95GB/hour when using modern hardware. Operating System: OS Independent.

43. Solr (http://lucene.apache.org/solr/)

Solr is an enterprise search platform based on the Lucene tools. It powers the search capabilities for many large sites, including Netflix, AOL, CNET and Zappos. Operating System: OS Independent.

Data Aggregation and Transfer

44. Sqoop (http://sqoop.apache.org/)

Sqoop transfers data between Hadoop and RDBMSes and data warehouses. As of March of this year, it is now a top-level Apache project. Operating System: OS Independent.

45. Flume (https://cwiki.apache.org/confluence/display/FLUME/Home;jsessionid=9D4FBF63843BF869325B486D0DEF0676)

Another Apache project, Flume collects aggregates and transfers log data from applications to HDFS. It's Java-based, robust and fault-tolerant. Operating System: Windows, Linux, OS X.

46. Chukwa (http://chukwa.apache.org/)

Built on top of HDFS and MapReduce, Chukwa collects data from large distributed systems. It also includes tools for displaying and analyzing the data it collects. Operating System: Linux, OS X.

Miscellaneous Big Data Tools

47. Terracotta (http://www.terracotta.org/)

Terracotta's "Big Memory" technology allows enterprise applications to store and manage big data in server memory, dramatically speeding performance. The company offers both open source and commercial versions of its Terracotta platform, Big

Memory, Ehcache and Quartz software. Operating System: OS Independent.

48. Avro (http://avro.apache.org/)

Apache Avro is a data serialization system based on JSON-defined schemas. APIs are available for Java, C, C++ and C#. Operating System: OS Independent.

49. Oozie (http://oozie.apache.org/)

This Apache project is designed to coordinate the scheduling of Hadoop jobs. It can trigger jobs at a scheduled time or based on data availability. Operating System: Linux, OS X.

50. Zookeeper (http://zookeeper.apache.org/)

Formerly a Hadoop sub-project, Zookeeper is "a centralized service for maintaining configuration information, naming, providing distributed synchronization, and providing group services." APIs are available for Java and C, with Python, Perl, and REST interfaces planned. Operating System: Linux, Windows (development only), OS X (development only)

Source: (http://www.datamation.com/data-center/50-top-open-source-tools-for-big-data-3.html

Chapter 4: BIG DATA: FACTS & FIGURES (APPLICATION, USE & BENEFITS)

This overview of big data application, use and benefits will help you to understand what is big data analytics, the business value it brings and how various types of organizations across different industries are applying it to address their unique business requirements.

What is big data analytics?

The definition of big data holds the key to understanding big data analytics. According to the Gartner IT Glossary, Big Data is high-volume, high-velocity and high-variety information assets that demand cost effective, innovative forms of information processing for enhanced insight and decision making.

Volume refers to the amount of data. Many factors are contributing to high volume: sensor and machine-generated data, networks, social media, and much more. Enterprises are awash with terabytes and, increasingly, petabytes of big data.

Variety refers to the number of types of data. Big data extends beyond structured data such as numbers, dates and strings to include unstructured data such as text, video, audio, click streams, 3D data and log files.

Velocity refers to the speed of data processing. The pace at which data streams in from sources such as mobile devices, clickstreams, high-frequency stock trading, and machine-to-machine processes is massive and continuously fast moving.

Like conventional analytics and business intelligence solutions, big data mining and analytics helps uncover hidden patterns, unknown correlations, and other useful business information. However, big data tools can analyze high-volume, high-velocity and high-variety information assets far better than conventional tools and relational databases that struggle to capture, manage, and process big data within a tolerable elapsed time and at an acceptable total cost of ownership.

Organizations are using new big data technologies and solutions such as Hadoop, MapReduce, <u>Hadoop Hive</u> (http://www.qubole.com/ resources/articles/hive-as-a-service/), Spark, Presto, Yarn, Pig, NoSQL databases and more to support their big data requirements.

What are the use cases for big data analytics?

 Marketing

- Campaign management and optimization
- Micro segmentation of consumers and markets
- Location-based marketing
- Cross-selling and up-selling
- Sentiment analysis
- One-to-one marketing
- 360-degree customer view

 Finance

- Risk management
- Fraud detection and prevention
- Wealth management
- Anti-money laundering
- Credit risk, scoring and analysis
- Trade surveillance

 Government

- Fraud and threat prediction and detection
- Cyber security
- Compliance and regulatory analysis

 Healthcare

- Patient care quality and outcomes analysis
- Reimbursement modeling
- Public health reporting
- Clinical data transparency
- Public health surveillance and response
- Clinical trial design and analysis

 Insurance

- Risk assessment and avoidance
- Claims fraud detection
- Call center workload analysis
- Telematics-optimized underwriting
- Customer value management
- Catastrophic planning

 Retail

- Merchandising and market basket analysis
- Supply chain management and analytics
- Loyalty program management
- Event/behavior based targeting
- Cross-channel customer service optimization

 Telecommunications

- Customer churn prevention
- Call detail record analysis
- Network planning and optimization
- Mobile user location analysis
- New product research and development

What are the benefits of big data analytics?

According to a survey of 540 enterprise decision makers involved in big data purchases by Webopedia's parent company Quin Street, about half of all respondents said they were applying big data and analytics to improve customer retention, help with product development and gain a competitive advantage. These are just a few of the actionable insights made possible by big data analysis. Whether an organization is looking to boost sales and marketing results, uncover new revenue opportunities, improve customer service, optimize operational efficiency, reduce risk, or drive other business results, big data insights can help.

The introduction of Big Data has given organizations access to more data than ever before. Unstructured data would have previously been considered 'dead' and of no value, but with Big Data it can be collected and analyzed in order to benefit organizations. Big Data gives organizations the opportunity to discover data correlations and patterns that before would have remained hidden. This means organizations now have access to more accurate information which can influence their business.

Big Data can provide benefits to your organization through ensuring that you have as much data as possible before making important business decisions. This will enable you to feel more confident when making business choices. The wealth of data available through Big Data also enables marketing strategies to be improved and more accurately targeted. This could help you to greatly increase your customer base, and push your organization ahead of the competition. Improvements in these areas of business can ultimately lead to an increase in revenue as your organization is able to both cut costs and attract more customers.

In summary, the benefits of Big Data include:

- More accurate data
- Improved business decisions
- Improved marketing strategy and targeting
- Increased revenue due to increased customer and base and decreased costs

http://www.e-dba.com/what_are_the_benefits_of_bigdata.html

Three big benefits of big data analytics

Google, eBay and LinkedIn were among the first to experiment with big data. They developed proof of concept and small-scale projects to learn if their analytical models could be improved with new data sources. In many cases, the results of these experiments were positive. Today, big data analytics is no longer just an experimental tool. Many companies have begun to achieve real results with the approach, and are expanding their efforts to encompass more data and models.

After interviewing more than 50 companies for a SAS-sponsored project called *"Big Data in Big Companies"*, **Tom Davenport (IIA Director of Research and faculty leader) reveals the true value of big data at work.** Here's how they're getting value:

1. Cost reduction: Big data technologies like Hadoop and cloud-based analytics can provide substantial cost advantages. While comparisons between big data technology and traditional architectures (data warehouses and marts in particular) are difficult because of differences in functionality, a price comparison alone can suggest order-of-magnitude improvements. Virtually every large company I interviewed, however, is employing big data technologies not to replace existing architectures, but to augment them. Rather than processing and storing vast quantities of new data in a data warehouse, for example, companies are using Hadoop clusters for that purpose, and moving data to enterprise warehouses as needed for production analytical applications. Well-established firms like City, Wells Fargo and USAA all have substantial Hadoop projects underway that exist alongside existing storage and processing capabilities for analytics. While the long-term role of these technologies in enterprise architecture is unclear, it's likely that they will play a permanent and important role in helping companies manage big data.

2. *Faster, better decision making:* Analytics has always involved attempts to improve decision making, and big data doesn't change that. Large organizations are seeking both faster and better decisions with big data, and they're finding them. Driven by the speed of Hadoop and in-memory analytics, several companies I researched were focused on speeding up existing decisions. For example, Caesars, a leading gaming company that has long embraced analytics, is now embracing big data analytics for faster decisions. The company has data about its customers from its Total Rewards loyalty program, web click streams, and real-time play in slot machines. It has traditionally used all those data sources to understand customers, but it has been difficult to integrate and act on them in real time, while the customer is still playing at a slot machine or in the resort.

Caesars has found that if a new customer to its loyalty program has a run of bad luck at the slots; it's likely that customer will never come back. But if it can present, say, a free meal coupon to that customer while he's still at the slot machine, he is much more likely to return to the casino later. The key, however, is to do the necessary analysis in real time and present the offer before the customer turns away in disgust with his luck and the machines at which he's been playing. In pursuit of this objective, Caesars has acquired Hadoop clusters and commercial analytics software. It has also added some data scientists to its analytics group.

Some firms are more focused on making better decisions analyzing new sources of data. For example, health insurance giant United Healthcare is using "natural language processing" tools from SAS to better understand customer satisfaction and when to intervene to improve it. It starts by converting records of customer voice calls to its call center into text and searching for indications that the customer is dissatisfied. The company has already found that the text analysis improves its predictive capability for customer attrition models.

3. New products and services: Perhaps the most interesting use of big data analytics is to create new products and services for customers. Online companies have done this for a decade or so, but now predominantly offline firms are doing it too. GE, for example, has made a major investment in new service models for its industrial products using big data analytics.

Verizon Wireless is also pursuing new offerings based on its extensive mobile device data. In a business unit called Precision Market Insights, Verizon is selling information about how often mobile phone users are in certain locations, their activities and backgrounds. Customers thus far have included malls, stadium owners and billboard firms. For the Phoenix Suns, an NBA basketball team, Verizon's Precision Market Insights offered information on where people attending the team's games live, what percentage of game attendees are from out of town, and how often game attendees combine a basketball game with a baseball spring training game or a visit to a fast food chain. Such insights are obviously valuable to the Suns in targeting advertising and promotions.

New Trends in Big Data and Data Science

- Posted by Vincent Granville (http://www.datasciencecentral. com/profile/VincentGranville) on November 11, 2014 at 10:30am
- View Blog (http://www.datasciencecentral.com/profiles/ blog/list?user= 3v6n5b6g08kgn)

This is based on requests from clients - vendors of data processing platforms and products - as well as trends in popular blogs, job postings, and my own reading. Here are a few topics recently gaining strong traction (items beyond #13 were recently added):

1. The rise of data plumbing, to make big data run smoothly, safely, reliably, and fast through all "data pipes" (Internet, Intranet, in-memory, local servers, cloud, Hadoop clusters etc.), optimizing redundancy, load balance, data caching, data storage, data compression, signal extraction, data summarization and more. We bought the domain name DataPlumbing.com last week.

2. The rise of the data plumber, system architect, and system analyst (a new breed of engineers and data scientists), a direct result of the rise of data plumbing.

3. Use of data science in unusual fields such as astrophysics, and the other way around (data science integrating techniques from these fields).

4. The death of the fake data scientist.

5. The rise of the right-sized data (as oppose to big data). Other keywords related to this trend are "light analytics", big data diet", "data outsourcing", the re-birth of "small data". Not that big data is going away, it is indeed getting bigger every second, but many

businesses are trying to leverage an increasingly smaller portion of it, rather than being lost in a (costly) ocean of unexploited data.

6. Putting more intelligence (sometimes called AI or deep learning) into rudimentary big data applications (currently lacking any true statistical science) such as recommendation engines, crowd sourcing or collaborative filtering. Purpose: detecting and eliminating spam, fake profiles, fake traffic, propaganda, attacks, scams, bad recommendations and other abuses, as early as possible.

7. Increased awareness of data security and protection, against computer or business hackers.

8. The rise of mobile data exploitation. For instance processing billions of text messages to detect the spread of a disease or other global risks, to help design alarm systems or market the right product in real-time (via opt-in, user-customized text messages) to a walking customer in a shopping mall. Not sure that even the NSA is capable of doing it as of today. The issue is more about capturing and reacting to the right signal, rather than absorbing/digesting big data. Another trend is optimization of revenue from mobile apps, leveraging mobile app dashboards.

9. The rise of the "automated statistician", in short, automated, scalable, robust analytic solutions fit for batch processing, real-time, machine-to-machine communications, and black-box analytics used by non-experts. More on this in our upcoming book, entitled data science 2.0.

10. Predictive modeling without models. Operations research and mathematicians contributing to the science of predicting, bringing mathematical optimization and simulation as an alternative to delicate and mysterious statistical models.

11. High performance computing (HPC) which could revolutionize the way algorithms are designed.

12. Increased collaboration between government agencies worldwide to standardize data and share it, for intelligence purposes. Imagine the census bureau sharing data with the IRS. Or banks in US sharing data with security agencies in Switzerland.

13. Forecasting space weather (best time / best location lo land on Mars), and natural events on Earth (volcanoes, Earthquakes, undersea weather patterns and implications to humans, when will Earth's magnetic field flip).

14. Use of data science for automated content generation (including content aggregation and classification); for automated correction of student essays; data science used in court to strengthen the level of evidence - or lack of - against a defendant; for plagiarism detection; for car traffic optimization and to compute optimum routes; for identifying, selecting and keeping ideal employees; for automated IRS audits sent to taxpayers to avoid costly litigation and time wasting; for urban planning; for precision agriculture.

15. Measuring yield of big data or data science initiatives (that is, benefit after software and HR costs, over baseline).

16. Digital health: diagnostic/treatment offered by a robot (artificial intelligence, decision trees) and/or remote doctors; digital law: same thing, with attorneys replaced by robots, at least for mundane cases or tasks. Even lawyers and doctors could have their jobs replaced by robots! This assumes that a lot of medical or legal data gets centralized, processed and made well structured for easy querying, updating and retrieval by (automated) deep learning systems.

17. Analytic processes (even in batch mode) accessible from your browser anywhere on any device. Growth of analytics apps and APIs.

Top 30 people in Big Data and Analytics

Innovation Enterprise has compiled a top 30 list for individuals in big data that have had a large impact on the development or popularity of the industry.

Here is an interesting list of top 30 people (actually 34) in Big Data & Analytics, created by Innovation Enterprise.

Unlike other lists, this is not based on Twitter or social media, but also on contributing directly to the industry, and focuses on those who had important parts to play in its growth and sustained popularity.

1. Doug   Cutting (https://en.wikipedia.org/wiki/Doug_Cutting) and Mike   Cafarella   (https://en.wikipedia.org/wiki/Doug_Cutting), for creating Hadoop

2. Sergey   Brin (https://en.wikipedia.org/wiki/Sergey_Brin)   and Larry   Page   (https://en.wikipedia.org/wiki/Larry_Page), founders of Google

3. Edward Snowden, NSA Whistleblower

4. Rob   Bearden   (http://hortonworks.com/about-us/management-team/), founder of Horton works

5. Kirk D. Borne (https://www.linkedin.com/in/kirkdborne), professor and co-creator of the field of astro informatics

6. Stephen Wolfram (https://en.wikipedia.org/wiki/Stephen_Wolfram), creator of Mathematica and Wolfram Alpha

7. Rich Miner (https://www.gv.com/team/rich-miner) co-founders of Android and a pioneer in the mobile space.

8. Jamie Miller (http://www.ge.com/about-us/leadership/profiles/jamie-s-miller), CIO at GE

9. DJ Patil (https://www.linkedin.com/in/dpatil), a data science pioneer, coined the term "data scientist" with Jeff Hammer bacher

10. Monica Rogati (https://www.linkedin.com/in/mrogati), VP of Data at Jawbone

11. Jeff Smith (https://www.linkedin.com/pub/jeff-smith/a/3a4/901?trk=pub-pbmap), CIO at IBM

12. Jeff Bezos (https://en.wikipedia.org/wiki/Jeff_Bezos), founder and CEO of Amazon

13. Andy Palmer (https://www.linkedin.com/in/andypalmer), co-founder and CEO of TamR

14. Gregory Piatetsky-Shapiro (https://en.wikipedia.org/wiki/Gregory_I._Piatetsky-Shapiro), co-founder of KDD and SIGKDD, KDnuggets President

15. Sverre Jarp (http://openlab.web.cern.ch/about/people/sverre-jarp), ex-CTO at CERN open lab

16. Tom Reilly (https://www.linkedin.com/in/tjreilly), CEO at Cloudera

17. Tom Davenport (https://en.wikipedia.org/wiki/Thomas_H._Davenport), thought leader and author in analytics and business process innovation

18. John Schroeder (https://www.mapr.com/blog/author/john-schroeder) and M. C. Srivas (https://www.linkedin.com/pub/m-c-srivas/1/b27/41b), co-founders of MapR

19. Scott Howe (https://www.linkedin.com/pub/scott-howe/20/864/8a), President and CEO at Acxiom

20. Hilary Mason (https://www.linkedin.com/in/hilarymason), was the Chief Scientist at Bitly, founder at Fast Forward Labs

21. Edwina Dunn and Clive Humby (http://www.humbyanddunn.com/), founders of Dunnhumby

22. Anmol Modan (https://www.linkedin.com/in/anmolmadan), co-founder and CEO at Ginger.io

23. Chris Towers (https://www.linkedin.com/in/towerschris), head of big data channel at Innovation Enterprise

24. Billy Beane (https://en.wikipedia.org/wiki/Billy_Beane), baseball coach that inspired Moneyball

25. Tim O'Reilly (https://en.wikipedia.org/wiki/Tim_O%27Reilly), owner of O'Reilly Media

26. Vadim Kutsyy (https://www.linkedin.com/in/kutsyy), head of Inc Data Lab at eBay

27. Warren Buffett (https://en.wikipedia.org/wiki/Warren_Buffett), renowned investor

28. Arijit Sengupta (https://www.linkedin.com/in/asengupta), CEO at BeyondCore

29. Gil Press (https://www.linkedin.com/in/gilpress), data science writer at Forbes

30. Paco Nathan (http://liber118.com/pxn/), well-known data blogger

http://www.kdnuggets.com/2015/02/top-30-people-big-data-analytics.html

References

[1] Andreas Weigend (http://www.weigend.com).

[2] The new data refineries: transforming big data into decisions. (Technology Services Industry Association blog, covering a talk by Andreas Weigend. 6 January 2014)

[3] Shanta Devarajan - Africa's statistical tragedy. (World Bank blog, 6 October 2011)

[4] Marcelo Giugale. Fix Africa's statistics. (*The World Post* 18 December 2012)

[5] Joseph Hellerstein - The commoditization of massive data analysis. (Blog on O'Reilly.com 19 November 2008)

[6] Data data everywhere. Kenneth Cukier interviewed for *The Economist* (25 February 2010)

[7] Emmanuel Letouzé. Big data for development: opportunities and challenges. (*UN Global Pulse*, May 2012)

[8] Big data, big impact: new possibilities for international development. (World Economic Forum, 2012)

[9]James Manyika and others - Big data: the next frontier for innovation, competition and productivity. (McKinsey Global Institute May 2011)

[10] Danah Boyd and Kate Crawford. Six provocations for Big Data. (*A Decade in Internet Time: Symposium on the Dynamics of the Internet and Society*, September 2011)

[11] The physical size of big data - Infographic by Domo. (14 May 2013)

[12] Christopher Frank. Improving decision making in the world of Big Data. (*Forbes,* 25 March 2012)

[13] Reinventing society in the wake of Big Data. A Conversation with Alex (Sandy) Pentland (Edge, 30 August 2012)

[14] Eric Bouillet and others - Processing 6 billion CDRs/day: from research to production (experience report) (http://dl.acm.org/citation.cfm?doid=2335484.2335513) pp. 264-67 in *Proceedings of the 6th ACM International Conference on Distributed Event-Based Systems* (2012)

[15] Social impact through satellite remote sensing: visualising acute and chronic crises beyond the visible spectrum. (*UN Global Pulse*, 28 November 2011)

[16] Michael Horrigan. Big Data: a perspective from the BLS. Column written for *AMSTATNEWS*, the magazine of the American Statistical Association (1 January 2013)

[17] Gary King. Big Data is not about the data! Presentation (Harvard University USA, 19 November 2013)

[18] Sanjeev Sardana Big Data: it's not a buzzword, it's a movement (*Forbes*blog, 20 November 2013)

[19] Melamed C. Development data: how accurate are the figures? (*The Guardian*, 31 January 2014)

[20] 2010 World population and housing census programme - United Nations Statistics Division.

[21] Laura Gray. How to boost GDP stats by 60% (*BBC News Magazine*, 9 December 2012)

[22] Nigeria's economy will soon overtake South Africa's (*The Economist*, 21 January 2014)

[23] The billion prices project. Massachusetts Institute of Technology

[24] Measuring economic sentiment (*The Economist*, 18 July 2012)

[25] Piet Daas and Mark van der Loo, Big Data (and official statistics) Working paper prepared for the Meeting on the Management of Statistical Information Systems - (23-25 April 2013)

[26] Rebecca Tave Gluskin and others - Evaluation of Internet-Based Dengue Query Data: Google Dengue Trends. (*PLOS Neglected Tropical Diseases*, 27 February 2014)

[27] Emilio Zagheni and others - Inferring international and internal migration patterns from Twitter data. (World Wide Web Conference, April 7-11, 2014, Seoul, Korea)

[28] New primer on mobile phone network data for development. (*UN Global Pulse*, 5 November 2013)

[29] Joshua Blumenstock and others - Motives for mobile phone-based giving: evidence in the aftermath of natural disasters (30 December, 2013)

[30] Michael Wu. Big Data Reduction 3: from descriptive to prescriptive. (Science of Social blog, Lithium 10 April 2013)

[31] Arvind Narayanan and Vitaly Shmatikov Robust de-anonymization of large sparse datasets; Pages 111-125 in Proceedings of the 2008 IEEE Symposium on Security and Privacy (IEEE Computer Society Washington, DC, USA 2008)

[32] Yves-Alexandre de Montjoye and others. Unique in the Crowd: The privacy bounds of human mobility (*Nature* scientific reports 25 March 2013)

[33] Erica Goode. Sending the police before there's a crime. (*The New York Times*, 15 August 2011)

[34] It is getting easier to foresee wrongdoing and spot likely wrongdoers (*The Economist*, 18 July 2013)

[35] Kate Crawford. Think again: Big Data. Why the rise of machines isn't all it's cracked up to be. (Foreign Policy, 9 May 2013)

[36] Neil M. Richards and Jonathan H. King - Three paradoxes of Big Data. (*Stanford Law Review*, 3 September 2013)

[37] Neil M. Richards and Jonathan H. King - Big Data ethics - (*Wake Forest Law Review*, 23 January 2014)

[38] Neil M. Richards and Jonathan H. King - Gigabytes gone wild (Aljazeera America, 2 March 2014)

[39] Rahul Bhargava. Toward a concept of popular data. (MIT Center for Civic Media, 18 November 2013)

[40] James Manyika and others. Open data: unlocking innovation and performance with liquid information (McKinsey Global Institute, October 2013)

[41] Emmanuel Letouzé. The Big Data revolution should be about knowledge security (Post-2015.org, 1 April 2014)

[42] Roy, Ajit Kumar 2015 - Applied Big Data Analytics: ASIN: B00Y95NV3A, Kindle Self Pubishing.Amazon

[43] Roy, Ajit Kumar.2015. 'Highlights on Big Data, Predictive Analytics and Business Intelligence Software' - *In A. K. Roy (Eds.) Emerging Technologies of 21st Century. NIPA, New Delhi*

http://www.sas.com/content/dam/SAS/en_us/doc/whitepaper2/bigdata-bigcompanies-106461.pdf

http://hbr.org/2013/12/analytics-30/ar/1

Ebook: Strategic Guide to Big Data Analytics (http://www.cio.com/article/2394947/business-intelligence/strategic-guide-to-big-data-analytics.html)

http://www.scidev.net/global/data/feature/big-data-for-development-facts-and-figures.html

ABOUT THE AUTHOR

Award winning Key Note Speaker at International Level, Professor Ajit Kumar Roy is an acclaimed researcher and consultant. Prof. Roy obtained his M.Sc. degree in Statistics and joined Agricultural Research Service (ARS) of Indian Council of Agricultural Research (ICAR) as a Scientist (Statistics) in 1976. In recent past was engaged as National Consultant (Impact Assessment), for East &North Eastern States of India at National Agricultural Innovation Project (World Bank funded) of ICAR. Prior to that he had served as a Consultant (Statistics) at Central Agricultural University, Agartala. Earlier had served at CIFA, ICAR, as Principal Scientist and was involved in applied research in the areas of ICT, Statistics, Bioinformatics Analytics, and Economics. At International level he served as a Computer Specialist at SAARC Agricultural Information Centre (SAIC), Dhaka, Bangladesh for over 3 years.

The author with over 45 years of research and teaching experience in Statistical Analysis, Analytics, and information & Knowledge management edited eighteen books and several conference proceedings. Besides, published over 100 articles in refereed journals. His recent best-sellers are 'Applied Big Data Analytics'; 'Impact of Big Data Analytics on Business, Economy, Health Care and Society'; 'Data Science - A Career Option for 21st Century';' Self Learning of Bioinformatics Online'; 'Applied Bioinformatics, Statistics and Economics in Fisheries Research' and 'Applied Computational Biology and Statistics in Biotechnology and Bioinformatics'. He served as a Member, Organizing Committee, Board for the 5th International Conference on 'Biometrics and Biostatistics' held during, October 20-21, 2016, Houston, Texas, USA. Editorial Board Member, Jacobs Journal of Biostatistics, Jacobs Publishers, 900 Great Hills, Trail # 150 w, Austin, Texas. He now works as Visiting Professor, question setter and examiner of four Indian Universities.

www.ingramcontent.com/pod-product-compliance
Lightning Source LLC
Chambersburg PA
CBHW060404290526
45791CB00002B/600